Yeah, My Dog Did That, Too

Erik's Adventures, reminding you of your dog's mischief, and why we love our dogs

J. B. Simms

Foreword by Capt. Joseph T. Simms

Copyright © 2017 by J.B. Simms
This edition published by Erik Publishing, and authorized by J.B. Simms.

All rights reserved. No part of the material protected by this copyright may be reproduced, or utilized in any form or by any means, electronic or mechanical, including photocopying, recording or by any informational storage system without written permission from the copyright owner. Printed in the United States of America.
Printed in the United States of America

```
Simms, J. B. (James B.), author.
Yeah, my dog did that, too: Erik's adventures, reminding you of
your dog's mischief, and why we love our dogs /
by J.B. Simms. pages cm
Includes bibliographical references.
ISBN 978-0-9795766-2-1 (paperback)
ISBN 978-0-9795766-3-8 (e-book)

 1. Erik (Dog), 1973-1987--Anecdotes.   2. Dogs--United  States-
    Biography--Anecdotes.  3. Simms, J. B. (James B.)--Family-
    Anecdotes.   4.  Human-animal  relationships--    Anecdotes.
    5. Biographies.  6. Anecdotes.   I. Title.

    SF426.2.S56 2017              636.70092'9

                                              QBI17-775
```

Contents

1- The College Puppy

2 -The Real Puppy Smell

3 -Housebreaking vs. Sleeping

4 -The First and Last Food Standoff

5- Gifts from Your Dog

6- The Police Ride-Along

7- The Slap Game

8- Bernie's Graduation Day

9- Dog- 'Napped and Rescued

10- Dog "on" a Blanket

11- Learning to Go Hide

12- The Christmas Tree

13- The Vaccination Clinic Fight

14- Dog Farts are Still Funny

15- Graduation Party

16- Not Sharing the Car Seat

17- These Chewed Shoes Don't Match

18- Beth Goes Flying

19- New Neighborhood: New Dog Fight

20- Call the Food Police

21- Just Drop the Leash

22- A Fence Is No Barrier

23- The Pecking Order

24- Neighbors Knew Your Dog First

25- Recognizing A "Doggie Bag"

26- An Amazing Instinct

27- Protecting the Neighbor's House

28- Dogs Learn to Open Doors

29- Calculated Revenge

30- Erik as the "Cookie Monster"

31- The Dog Pound and the Bank

32- Protection Game

33- Protecting Joe and Fridge Food

34- A Hospital Visit

35 – A Dog Plans a Covert Attack

36- Eating in the Car

37 – Caged

38 –The Dog Behind the Bus

39 – Erik Attacks my Tie

40 – Getting Older-Sad Signs

41 - The Last Days

42- Dogs Teach Us How to Love

Acknowledgements

I would like to name some of Erik's friends; Orbit (female Springer Spaniel, owned by my closest friends Tom and Laurette Burdyl), Pluto (Orbit's son), neighbor dog Rebel (nasty fights), Zeus (who taught Erik that a dog must fight to have a girlfriend, and who belonged to my lovely friend, Mari Gramling), Sugar (a girlfriend of Erik's and mother to some of his kids), and a slew of unnamed girlfriends. Tom and Laurette always treated Erik as one of their own, keeping him from time to time. I must mention my cousin Pam Lominac, whose son John screamed when he had a cookie taken from his mouth by Erik. Erik paid her back for throwing him out of my house by digging a 3-foot hole in her back yard when we visited Pam.

I thank my son Joe, and his expectant wife Julie Dioguardi Simms, who did edits and photo work. This book will be their daughter's first book. My friend, book publisher Dianne Helm, gave me great edit advice. Alexandra Camazine, my SoCal editor, was a valuable contributor. I thank Beth James, Joe's mom and my former wife. Beth did not grow up with a dog, but after having Erik around for a year and a half in college, and afterward with my years of immaturity, Joe growing up, and Erik into everything, those who knew her referred to her as "Saint Beth". Erik loved her as well.

Preface

We love dog stories because most of us have had a dog in our life. There is nothing more comforting than having a dog read your mood, sit next to you, or nudge your hand.

Almost all entertaining dog stories are a result of something your dog did when the dog was off the leash, being free and spontaneous. Some people brag that their dog is so smart or so cute, blah, blah, blah. My dog was smart, but too big to be called cute. He was a mix between a collie and a German Shepherd, and must have been a bit of Border Collie.

When people tell a dog story, someone will always respond to a story with trying to "one up" the person. This is not a book about comparing our dogs; this book reveals how similarly our dogs act, and how we react to their behavior. These stories bond real dog people. This is the reason for this book; to let you know that dogs do the same "stuff".

Times have changed. Dogs are not allowed to be loose, spontaneous, and have "dog fun". They cannot run off for hours with one of their friends to play unless the dog lives in a rural area. The neighbor's dog does not show up on your doorstep looking for your dog to come out and play. That used to happen. I always thought it was cool to see someone's dog in my yard when I was a kid. The dog was looking for my dog. The dog-park, or "bark-park" does not count. Dogs know their owners are nearby and know they will get caught if they misbehave.

This book is about Erik, who was with me from 1973-1987. He lived with me, a college roommate named Bernie Vitti (off campus apartment), my wife (Beth), and my son (Joe). He also lived with roommates after my divorce. I first got him while I was attending a small college in northwest South Carolina. Many of the stories you will read have descriptions of things Erik did, along with quotes from persons who were at the scene of the story.

There were few fences for dogs, most leash laws either did not exist or were not enforced, and dogs ran free in neighborhoods. It was that way in the 50's and 60's when I grew up in north central Florida. Dogs ran free. They visited different houses. They visited different dogs. They went to the houses where the people would give treats to a neighborhood dog, or water if it was available. They pooped in other people's yards (not in their own). Dogs were like kids; out running around but would come home when they were hungry or when they wanted to sleep.

When we were kids, we knew the names of the dogs in the neighborhood, just like we knew the names of our friends and their parents. Little yappy dogs did not venture far from their home but the bigger dogs would end up a mile away from home, especially if there was a female dog in "heat". These dogs had personality. We knew the dogs, their "families," and the dogs knew us.

The dogs had fun like the rest of us. I hate to see that spontaneous fun taken from a dog's life, but those of us who are old enough do remember the days when you would open a door for your dog to go outside and not have a concern for his safety. The dog would go to the door because he had to go "out" or maybe just wanted out of the house because he was bored. Rarely would we go looking for our dog.

I am going to share stories about Erik. Friends and acquaintances of mine have heard many of the stories, many were involved in the stories, and it is a running joke with some about the Erik stories. After Erik was about a year old, I realized that I was living with a dog who acted like a 13-year-old kid; he created his fun, getting into trouble, having that look on his face like he was denying involvement in something (mostly paternity), and doing the same things a 13-year-old boy did or wanted to do.

Our dogs make us laugh, make us angry, embarrass us, make us clean up after them, make impolite noises, have a strange aroma, but they will also come up to you, unannounced, and lick your hand. All was forgiven, and forgotten, or so they thought.

I named him Erik as a tribute to one of my college professors Dr. Dennis Erickson, and a reminder of the aggravation of being in his classes. Thirty years after college graduation, I found Dr. Erickson to tell him about my first book. The conversation began with me identifying myself, telling him that I was in his classes during the early 1970's. Dr. Erickson replied, "I remember you. You named your dog after me."

Erik would go to class with me, and he went into classes I did not attend. Most professors tolerated him walking into a class, and many people knew his name. He wandered around like the other dogs in the small college town, but only a few dogs had the guts to enter the door of a lecture building and go into a class.

Once, Erik entered an auditorium where I gave announcements to the student body. I did not know he was offstage in the wings until I heard people backstage laughing. I looked to my left, Erik saw me, then he walked out on stage. I told him to sit, and he sat next to me until I finished, and he followed me off stage. I was married then, and everyone laughed except for Beth and the faculty. Beth told me that one of her professors asked her if I was her husband.

Erik had his photograph taken for the yearbook with a fraternity of which I was not a member. He also was in my college graduation photo, with my wife.

We are glad our dogs had fun experiences. They deserved to have fun, not just being put into a crate and let out to amuse us. They deserved to have lives independent from us.

We miss family members, but do not get emotional thinking of missing the family member the same way we miss our dog. It is different. Dogs never say anything to hurt your feelings. Dogs do not betray you. Dogs do not have a stressful day and come home with a bad attitude. Dogs do not tell stories about their friends or their owners.

The best feeling is to be able to look at your dog, without speaking, and your dog can see from your face that you do love the dog. You can also see the look on your dog's face when he is telling you that he loves you. That is why we have a dog.

Foreword

When my dad told me he was going to write a book full of stories about our dog Erik I thought, "Well, that makes sense." I grew up hearing these stories and anyone who spent time with Dad in the last 40 years would have also heard a story or two about Erik.

This book will take you through almost 14 years of a dog's life. From being the last of the litter to be picked, becoming a companion and friend to a small college town, and finally a big brother to me, Erik certainly lived a great dog's life.

Most people are familiar with the tales about a boy and his dog, but this one is a little different. My dad found Erik in a pivotal time in his life when he was about to graduate college and start a family. My dad and Erik grew up and entered adulthood together. Erik and my dad drank beer at parties, protected each other from real or perceived threats, and showed each other unconditional love.

While I was too young to fully appreciate most of these stories since Erik was already 5 years old when I came along, I understood immediately that he was part of the family.

Some of my first memories are of my dad and me going to the football or baseball fields near our house and Erik was always there with us. Erik was my guest for show and tell when I was in kindergarten, he served as a pillow for me when I was 7 and got the chicken pox, and he was there when I learned to ride a bike.

Throughout this book my dad compares Erik to a 13-year-old son. The dog had a sense of humor, created his own fun and was headstrong just like a teenager. Sometimes kids disappoint, test the boundaries, and aggravate us and so do our dogs. Everyone that has cleaned up after a dog then has them come and lick your face knows what I'm talking about.

When I was growing up with Erik, I thought everyone else with a dog had the same experiences. It wasn't until I was older that I realized Erik was one of a kind, but at the same time, these are stories to which all dog owners and dog lovers can relate.

This book is not only a way for dog owners and dog lovers to reminisce about some of their own experiences, but it's a way to honor a family member.

That's what this book is about; family. While Erik is the focus of the stories, every one of these memories has something to do with Erik's interaction with family or friends, except for the one where he got into the trashcan.

But at the heart of it, the book is a way to celebrate a member of the family.

Capt. Joseph T. Simms, USAF

Chapter One: The College Puppy

Midway through my junior year of college, I accumulated enough credit hours to enable me to live off campus. I knew I was going to move into a tiny apartment with my friend Bernie Vitti, an Italian from New Jersey. Bernie was a big strong guy, and sometimes acted like he just stepped off the boat at Ellis Island. Before I moved in with Bernie, a girl named Rachel made an announcement at school that she had a box of puppies to be adopted. Bernie gave me permission to bring a puppy to the apartment when I moved in. Bernie had no idea what he was in for.

I went to Rachel's apartment to see the puppies. There were at least five puppies. I picked one out and told Rachel I would be back in a day or so to pick him up. Two days later, after I finished my exams (probably around December 19, 1973), I went to get the dog I had chosen. Rachel told me there was only one left. Was I getting the runt? Not necessarily, but he was the last one. He seemed healthy so I took him.

Fall exams ended, and I drove from college in South Carolina to Florida on the same evening that I picked up the puppy. I put the puppy into my 1966 Mustang and down the road I went.

The puppy would be named Erik. I named him for a professor of mine, Dennis Erikson.

The puppy, a male, was about 6-8 weeks old. He did not whine, which I thought was good. He was on the floor of the passenger side, crawled up onto the seat, past the gear-shifter, and onto my lap. He tried to crawl up into my face. He then crawled toward the driver door where I was resting my left arm. He balanced himself, with my help, onto my forearm and fell asleep on top of my arm as my arm was leaning against the armrest.

How the hell can that be comfortable? The bond began; he trusted me that I would not move my arm and let him fall.

Do you remember having a puppy in your car, especially on a long trip? What a pain it was to have to stop and walk the dog in the grass at a gas station, or have him crawl under your feet as you tried to drive. You could not leave the puppy alone in for very long because he would find something to chew.

Do you also remember the first bonding experience with your dog, when you locked eyes?

Chapter Two: The Real Puppy Smell

A day or so after the Christmas holiday, I drove a U-Haul truck from Tampa, Florida back to college. I had stuff to put into my apartment, and a piece of furniture for Beth, my wife-to-be. It was probably a 12-hour drive. The plan was to stop from time to time, let Erik walk in the grassy areas of gas stations and areas to stop, let the people say "Oh, what a cute dog, blah blah blah". It was going to be fun. He was going to be a buddy. He would obey me. I would teach him tricks. He would become housebroken quickly, never eat my clothes, and eat the food I gave him. Erik had other plans.

After about 6 hours on the road I stopped and got something to drink and eat. I took Erik out to do the walk thing, and he did the "squat to pee" since he did not know how to lift his leg. We got back into the big truck, and down the road we went.

Erik was sleeping on the floor of the passenger side. There was a lot of room. A makeshift water bowl was there. As I drove, tootling on the radio, something started burning my nose. I looked over to see Erik walking in a circle around a pile of dog poop he just made. The look on his face was, "What?"

"I just put you out, in the grass, and you wait until now to do this?"

I was trying to drive on the interstate, roll down a window, and keep the dog from walking in that pile Erik created which was a pungent as mace. I was trying not to puke. It was so bad I could not drive.

I pulled off the interstate, cleaned the floor, the dog, and now myself. I was not prepared for this. I had to stop further down the road and find something to wash the floor, and get the smell off me.

I was thinking, "I am going to kill this dog." I felt like the people who chose the puppies ahead of Erik were psychic. Erik was going to be trouble. The prospective dog owners looked at Erik's face and "knew" he was trouble. This dog was going to be God's joke on me.

Do you remember when your puppy left you a very smelly present in the car and you had to stop and clean it up before you could drive any further?

Chapter Three: Housebreaking vs. Sleeping

I had not seen a crate for dogs in 1973. I am not a fan of a dog crate. Some dogs think it is their home, their little plastic wired domain, but that is just uncomfortable for me to watch.

The apartment I had with my New Jersey Italian friend (Bernie) was very small. We had some very big parties; it was college, and it is what you do. Most days I just wanted to crash in my bed and not have to attend to a puppy.

There are some things everyone should experience, and one is having a puppy at night. I put Erik in a cardboard box next to my bed. Erik kept moving around in the box. He got up on his back legs and started clawing at my mattress. I put my hand off the edge of the bed and into the box for him to play with my hand as I tried to sleep. By now Bernie is telling me the dog is whining. I can hear the dog because he is right next to me. Bernie started cursing in Italian. It was worth it to hear Bernie get aggravated because he was hilarious when he was agitated.

"Duke (my nickname I had from college), the dog, it's making noise." Bernie had such a strong Italian accent that I had to laugh at him.

My hand was still in the box. I was trying to sleep, or pass out, so I hoped Erik would play with my hand while I slept. Erik started chewing on my hand. Then he tried to climb out of the box, and started that whining stuff again. Some people put a puppy far away and let them crap or pee in the box. I thought I would rather lose sleep than clean up anything like what he did in that truck.

I was thinking I had to take him outside but it was cold outside. It was January in northwest South Carolina, and the temperature was probably in the low 30's. I got up, grabbed Erik and took him out to his spot. "Over here, come on, get back here, come on, DO SOMETHING!" Rushing a dog to have a bowel movement is a waste of time. The look they give you says, "Let me see you do this and see how you feel."

We all take the puppy to their "spot" for them to pee and poop because the "spot" smells like poop and that is what you want them to do, poop. It is the power of suggestion. It was probably 3:30am and it was cold and raining; raining a lot. I had to find an umbrella and watch Erik play across the yard as I directed him to his "spot". It is what you had to do, and you did it. You will find out the puppy had crawled out of the box and left you another smelly pile, and the smell will wake you.

We do this "take the dog to the spot" dance and hope the dog goes to the spot, does his business, goes back inside and goes to sleep. "Hell no; you want to play." Eventually he did his thing and he went to his box. I went to the liquor cabinet for a shot to help me get back to sleep.

It is always so nice when puppies slept through the night. It sounds like I am talking about a human baby. We say things to the dog we would not say to a human, but believe me, they understand.

Do you remember taking the puppy out in nasty weather, at all hours, to house-break the puppy?

Chapter Four: The First and Last Food Standoff

Puppies need to be fed every 4 hours or so. Erik was no exception. My class load was not heavy that semester, but I had some hard classes and studied a lot. Moving off campus allowed me to study more (Calculus) and my classes were spread out so I was able get back to feed Erik.

He was getting better about going out. I had to barricade the kitchen in our apartment when Erik was very young, not leaving him outside while I was gone until he was probably 5 months old.

One morning I came back to feed him at around 11am. I put the dry food into the bowl and put the hot water into the bowl. The food needed to sit for a minute and soak into the food, and cool off. I put the bowl on the floor. Erik wanted his food "now" but I had to move the bowl of hot food before Erik ate. The food was too hot. Erik put his nose into the bowl. I reached down to pick up the bowl and that dog, probably 3 months old, leaned back on his back legs, looked at me, and gave out the nastiest growl you could hear from a puppy.

I lost it. He was standing close enough to me that I reached out with my foot, placed it behind his front legs, and slid him across the kitchen floor and into a wall, which was about 10 feet away. After hitting that wall, Erik got up, looked at me with glazed eyes and I told him, "If you ever try that again, ..." I moved the bowl and he walked sheepishly to the bowl and had his lunch. He never did that again. I could move his bowl anytime I wished from then on. Lesson learned.

He was not hurt, so stop making those faces as you read this.

By God, I was going to be the alpha dog in this relationship from then on, or so I thought. Dogs have long memories.

Do you remember your dog challenging you as the alpha dog in the house?

Chapter Five: Gifts from Your Dog

Dogs, mostly young ones, bring you prizes. They want to show you how smart they are and they bring their prey to you. They want your approval.

I had a female dog, after Erik, who would go out into the neighborhood and bring me the neighbor's newspaper. One Saturday morning I had 6 newspapers on my front porch. I looked out the door and there she was, my dog on the porch, sitting with the newspapers surrounding her. I knew what had happened.

I looked out into the street and saw a Volkswagen bug having a magnetic sticker on the door. Oh, my God, it was the newspaper delivery person, redelivering the papers my dog had stolen. I grabbed the dog, put her inside, grabbed up all the newspapers, put them inside, and stayed inside for a while.

The next day my dog brought me the Sunday paper from the neighbor's front porch, dragging the huge paper across the street. I gathered up the paper and took it back to the pretty lady across the street. Chivalry, right? Well, she was pretty.

That dog also would bring me squirrels she had caught and killed, and put them on the porch.

When Erik was about 5 months old and old enough to be out alone in the rural college town, he brought a present to Bernie and me which will never be forgotten.

Erik had a cardboard box set up for him at the front door of the apartment. The apartment was a duplex, and there was a concrete entryway at the front door behind a brick wall. Erik could sleep in the box (one side was cut out) in the shade while Bernie and I were in class.

From time to time I found Erik had brought me sticks, spoons, plastic dishes, rusty cans, and all sorts of "presents" he thought he would bring home. On this spring day, he brought home the classic present: a rotten fish head.

I came back to the apartment after class and a most foul smell hit me about 50 feet from my front door. As I approached the entryway, Erik was lying in his box, next to a fish head which was about the size of a dinner plate. Erik looked up at me, I looked at the fish head, and I about gagged.

I realized he had traveled through the small patch of woods behind the duplex and found the food garden which belonged to the town chief of police. The chief fished quite a bit, and buried remains of fish in his garden as fertilizer. I guess I learned that Erik had a hell of a sense of smell. He dug up the fish head and carried it back to our apartment. Can you picture a puppy carrying a rotten fish head?

I had two things to do: get rid of the fish head, which smelled worse than anything I ever smelled, and bathe Erik, who smelled like that rotten fish head. You should have heard Bernie, "Duke, what's that smell? It's a fish head."

Somehow, I bathed the nasty dog. Remember your dog getting into nasty trash, poop, or anything, rolling in it, having it caked on their hair, and you having to clean the dog?

The story continued. After I bathed Erik, I thought I would go to the student recreation center and get my mail. The trip was a few blocks, very little traffic, and Erik was becoming obedient enough that he had begun to listen to me. Erik was off the leash (which was normal) and off we went, walking together. I saw a student named Sybil Coghill sitting on a raised concrete walkway with her feet on the ground. Sybil held Erik while I got my mail. When I came back I chatted with Sybil for a minute or so, then Erik began heaving. You know, the dog-puke-heave? Erik was standing next to Sybil's feet, and there it came. Erik puked on Sybil's feet, and she was wearing leather sandals. The smell of the puke was the same as the dead fish. It became apparent that Erik had eaten some of the dead, rotten fish, it made him sick and he puked on Sybil's uncovered foot.

I don't remember what I said to Sybil. I believe she just left and went to a restroom. Funny, I never spoke much to Sybil after that.

Do you remember the crazy stuff your dog brought home?

Do you remember having to bathe a dog who had an aroma from hell all over him?

Do you remember the dog puke, that "yacking" sound, as you start looking for a door?

Yeah, My Dog Did That, Too

Chapter Six: The Police Ride-Along

It was a Saturday night. Beth and I had gone to a party and we returned to my apartment after the party. Erik was not home. I was not concerned, but Beth wanted me to go find him. Beth was a sweetheart; she did not want anyone to think she was too attached to Erik, but she was. Since I had just returned from the party, I was in no condition to be driving anywhere (I did drive home but that was different, right?) so I walked Beth back to her dorm and I commandeered a bicycle. It was not pretty sight; drunk college student on a bike.

I rode the bike to the main street in town, and arrived at the area where the two gasoline stations in town were across the street from one another. Butch Sain (who will be in a later story) owned the small Gulf station, and the Kennedy's (who will figure in the same story with Butch) owned the Exxon station. I saw a county police car in the parking lot of Kennedy's Exxon and the cop was sitting in the idling police car. In my attempt to construct complete sentences, I asked the cop if he had seen Erik, which I described to the cop. The cop told me that he had picked up Erik an hour or so earlier and Erik rode in the police car around the county for at least an hour. The cop said he brought him back a few minutes before I found the cop, and dropped him off at the same gasoline station where he picked up Erik.

The cop just told me that my dog approached him at the gas station, and jumped into the cop car. The cop took Erik on a "ride along" with the cop. That was cool, but still could not find Erik.

I rode the "borrowed" bike back to my apartment, and I found Erik lying in his cardboard box, waiting for me to return from the party. I guess he thought I would have gotten home later so I would have never known he went joy riding with a cop.

Our dogs kept their mischief secret. We never know where they have been, what they have done (unless someone told us), or who saw them. Your dog did that too; disappeared for a while and never told you what mischief they had committed.

Do you remember friends and neighbors telling you things about your dog which you did not know, and having seen your dog at places you had never been?

Chapter Seven: The Slap Game

Erik was feisty and very confident. He loved to play, and sometimes he liked it a big rough. It was a test for him. He enjoyed being taunted, and he would do things to let you know that he would tolerate only a limited amount of taunting. Many times, he would latch on to the bottom part of my pants, near my shoes, and tug my pants. My jeans had holes near the bottom of the legs where Erik had made holes or torn the jeans. I would see him on the college campus and he would greet me. When I walked away, maybe going to class (maybe) he would start tugging my pants leg as though he wanted me to continue to give him attention or just play with him. Many people played with him.

We devised a game I called the "slap game" which we played until his last days. Here is how it worked:

Erik would face me. I would lean over a bit, raise my hands near my face, and the palms of my hands would be facing one another, as in a martial art pose. I then began to taunt the dog. Erik was having none of that. Erik squatted in an aggressive pose and began growling as if he wanted to bite me. He had a very ferocious growl, and was quite a vicious fighter. I would taunt him verbally, and then playfully swing my hands near his face, eventually popping his nose with one of my hands. Eventually, Erik would lunge at me.

Once I gave him the gentle pop on the nose, he would become more aggressive. As he lunged at me, my job was to avoid him as he tried to bite my arm, hand, leg, or any particle of clothing. If I could pop him 10 times before he latched on or bit me, I would win. If not, he would win.

After the session, he would sit (on command), hand me alternate paws as if we were shaking hands, then I would lean over and he would lick my face. The game was over.

I used this slap game to alert persons how vicious Erik could be, but I knew Erik would not bite anyone (he never did). I knew he would not bite me viscously, but others did not. If I alerted him to something, he would growl. I could make him growl on command. It was disconcerting to others, but to Erik and me, it was a game, and he played it well. It was almost like a code; if I needed him to act aggressively, I simply used the tone of my voice.

Do you remember having our dogs react to a command of protection, or make a verbal command to bring something to their attention?

Chapter Eight: Bernie's Graduation Day

By May of 1974, Erik was about 7 months old, and almost an adult dog. He, and many of the dogs in town, roamed freely. Some of the free roaming dogs were his siblings which were in the same box in which I found Erik. I liked seeing Erik and the dogs out with their "friends" running free. Dogs need independence, have their own fun without humans messing things up.

Bernie's parents and his young sister came to South Carolina from New Jersey for Bernie's graduation. Both his parents were born in Italy. They brought more food than they did clothes, and they shared it with me. Erik got his share of Italian food scraps. Bernie's sister played with Erik.

On graduation day, Beth and I went to see Bernie and our other friends graduate. Beth and I would graduate the next year.

It was a warm day in May; a typical Southern day. The graduation area was a grassy area between two dormitories which faced each other. A large grassy communal area separated the dormitories. Many folding chairs were set up, and there was a wide path between the two sections of chairs. The podium was on a raised stage and placed right in the middle, facing the 10-foot wide grassy area between the two sections. Beth and I sat on the left side, facing the podium. I sat immediately on the isle, approximately twenty rows from the front.

The music began. To our right, and past the section of chairs, we could see the guy holding the scepter, leading the faculty to the stage. I could see the steps going up to the stage because the front seats were empty before graduates and faculty were seated. I started hearing laughter and snickering. As the scepter guy arrived near the stage, I saw why people were laughing; Erik was walking head of the procession. I glanced to my left, Beth gave me that look (guys, you know the "look") and she told me to go get him. I could not "get him" because Erik was at the front of the graduation procession.

People started calling his name, "Erik, Erik, come here, come on..." as they were trying to get him away from the procession and down the aisle. Finally, he walked into the aisle. Again, I was about 20 rows from the stage. I began the loud whisper trying to get his attention. Then he saw me. I made the "come on" hand gesture and walked to me as if nothing was wrong, tail up, mouth open as though he was simply enjoying his life.

I took off my belt and looped it into his collar. Erik sat with Beth and me throughout the graduation. I knew not to look back at Beth, because she was still giving me that "look". I was trying not to laugh as I sat petting Erik. It is still funny, and I am sure she is still annoyed with us both.

This would not be the last time Erik showed up unannounced.

Do remember when your dog showed up unexpectedly?

Chapter Nine: Dog-'Napped and Rescued

During the summer of 1974, I was away from the college town from June through July doing military training, so I left Erik in my apartment with a friend, Richard Spencer. Richard was supposed to feed Erik and basically take care of him while Richard attended summer school classes. No big job, so I thought.

About four weeks after I left, I got a letter from Beth that Erik was missing. Beth was very upset. She put an ad on local radio station. She really showed that she loved Erik but was not going to admit it. Beth never had a dog. Her dad would not let her family have a dog, but Erik could visit when I came to the house. Her dad was good about that.

It was odd that Erik was missing. He always came back to the apartment even though he walked freely around town. Although he was attached to me, he knew Richard, and I never thought he would just run off or go looking for me.

A month or so later before I returned to South Carolina, Richard told me that Erik had enjoyed the parties at the apartment, and some guy was giving him beer. Erik was having more fun than me. My dog was now ready for a 12-step program.

I returned on Friday, August 2, and Beth picked me up at the airport. We drove back to the college town to see our new apartment. We were getting married in a couple of weeks and would be spending our senior year as a married couple.

She was very upset that Erik was gone. I did not know what to say.

As we drove toward the college town, about 4 miles from town, I looked to my left and saw what appeared to be Erik in the front yard of a house. I stopped and Erik jumped right into my car. The guy there said that this dog was his dog; he said that he was a painter and the dog got into his truck while he was painting dormitories at the college. Erik had gone home with the painter?

I knew the painter was not going to hurt Erik, and I had no place for Erik at that time. I made as peaceful an exit as I could and let him know I would be back.

During the next week, I made a few telephone calls to the painter. He would not give up the dog. I filed a claim and delivery with the local magistrate. I was getting angry. I was getting married on August 17. I drove past the house a dozen or so times and did not see Erik. I even stopped to talk to the guy again but he still claimed the dog was his.

The Friday before I was getting married on Saturday, people from out of state were arriving for the wedding. I traveled to our new apartment, 45 miles away, to do some things when the phone rang. Thankfully, Beth had the phone connected. They guy who had Erik was on the phone. He said I could come get Erik.

You have no idea how happy I was.

The painter lived on a two-lane highway about three miles from our new apartment in the college town. I had to drive past his house to get back to Beth's house and I looked at his house every time I drove by after Erik became missing.

I drove into the driveway and the painter was standing at the front of his house with Erik on a leash. Erik was filthy. The guy had penned him under the house so I would not get him. I gave the guy $40.00 for feeding him, and put that dirty dog into my car. It did not matter; I had Erik.

I had only had Erik for about 7 months, but the bond was there.

After picking him up, I drove to Beth's parent's house. I got married the next day. Erik stayed with Beth's parents, and her mother Mary bathed Erik while Beth and I were on our honeymoon. I will always remember that Beth's mother did that for me.

Back from the honeymoon, the three of us drove back to experience another year of college. I knew that Beth was going to give me that dirty look a few more times. She had no idea what she was in for.

Erik would go missing more times, but for varied reasons.

Do you remember the first time your dog was lost, and the thought you would never see your dog again?

Chapter Ten: Dog "on" a Blanket

Beth figured out she was married to a kid who had a dog. She put up with a lot, and I had to give her credit. She yelled at me (deservedly so) and Erik (he was in trouble as I was) but there were times when she could not deny her affection for him.

Remember in college when the girls would lie out in the sun to get tan so they would look nice for us guys? Beth did that even after we were married. She would take a blanket and put it on the ground around the corner of the building, away from the road where my friends were driving.

I came home one day, probably after a class (like I went to class...) and there they were; Beth was out on the blanket, and Erik was lying there as the guard dog. It was not like his hair would get tanned, but he just went where the people were.

Erik had been doing this with the girls before Beth and I were married. He would travel across a road onto the Women's Campus and "lay out" with the girls.

I could see the affection between Erik and Beth. It was warm feeling to see their bond since she never had a dog when she was young. Erik could see that Beth was quiet by nature, and he reacted differently to her than he did me. It is interesting to see your dog act differently to other persons, as we act differently to different persons. Little did Beth know Erik would use that niceness as leverage for the mischief he was going to commit for the next decade.

Do you remember when your dog bonded differently with other members of your family?

J.B. Simms

Chapter Eleven: Learning to Go Hide

Erik, me, Ed Wehmeyer, and Ed's son.
It was winter, 1974. The buildings were married student apartments.

We were a young married college couple, with a dog. There was not a lot of money to go around. I was running the intramural program at school and getting paid. Occasionally, Beth and I went to eat at an Amish restaurant called Yoders, located in Abbeville, SC, which was about 12 miles from our apartment. I had to come back and referee football games so we had to return before 7:00pm. We decided to leave Erik in the apartment, alone. You know where this is story is going, don't you?

The apartment was one of those red brick government apartments, and when you open the back door, you could see straight through the apartment to the front door.

As you entered the apartment via the kitchen door, you could walk through the kitchen into the next room, which was the living room. If you continued to walk straight, you would walk out the front door. We parked at the back door which opened to the kitchen. The two small bedrooms and the bathroom were on the right as you passed through the kitchen. Knowledge of the layout is important for other stories to follow.

We pulled up to the back door of the apartment after having supper at the restaurant. As I unlocked the door, pushed the door open, I looked about 10 feet into the kitchen and saw the trash can on the floor, and the bag had been pulled out. All hell was about to break out.

I stepped in and looked past the trash can, and saw a trail of trash leading into the living room. A large piece of the trash bag was in the middle of the living room floor. It was very quiet. I took another step into the kitchen and then it happened; Erik's head popped up from the opposite side of the bag of garbage in the living room and he looked me straight in the eye. Time stood still. He knew the front door behind him was closed, so he could not get to the screen door to get out. He was caught. In a split second, you could see him thinking how to escape. I yelled at Beth to close the kitchen door.

I looked to my right and grabbed the discipline tool; a rolled newspaper with duct tape on one third of it for grip. Erik knew why the newspaper was there, he had seen it before. Most of the time I would just slap it on my hand or let him see it. This time was serious. It was dog killing time.

The trash can was full when we left the apartment to go eat. Of course, there was chicken in the trash; we lived in South Carolina. At the time, I was not concerned about the safety of Erik eating a chicken bone and hurting his throat. I was going to kill him. Trash was all over the kitchen. It was nasty, wet, rotten, smelly, vegetables, table scraps, coffee grounds, dirty Kleenex, and anything else you can imagine. Trash had been dragged into the living room.

When I grabbed the taped newspaper, the chase was on. Erik turned toward the front door, then tried to get past me into the kitchen. The kitchen door leading outside was shut and he knew he could bolt out that screen door, but not today. I stopped him and chased him past the two lounge chairs in the living room (that is all the sitting furniture we had) and then he darted toward the bedrooms. There I saw more trash in the hallway and in the bedrooms. This was going to be a dead, dead dog.

He ran into the bedroom. He ran past the bed and then came back toward me. Our eyes met again. All the time I am swinging and cussing. Beth is behind me somewhere but I never saw her. I was going to get that dog. Erik was darting back and forth so quickly that I had to laugh at myself because I could not catch him.

When Erik came back toward me he turned left and dove under the bed. I leaned over and started swinging the newspaper at him from under the bed but I could not reach him. I kept swinging and he kept backing up, knowing I could not reach him. I was yelling, "You better go hide, I will kill you. You hide right there. Go hide."

Erik was probably about 10-11 months old when that happened. He knew better than to get into the trash, but he was a dog.

From that day forward, and for the rest of his days, if he ever got into trouble, or was annoying or aggravating, all I had to say was, "go hide" and he would calmly walk into the bedroom of any house in which I was living and crawl under the bed.

Do you remember when your dog turned over the trash and dragged it all over the house?

J.B. Simms

Chapter Twelve: The Christmas Tree

This was going to be my first Christmas being married. I had my family; a wife and a dog, and very little money. We had no Christmas tree, but I was going to fix that.

I took a hatchet and got into my 1966 Mustang (nothing special about it back then) and drove to the woods. Somehow after chopping down an 8-foot pine tree, I tied it to the roof of my car and drove home. Yep, the husband brings home the tree to the little wife.

I brought the tree in the back door and saw that the front door open. There was always a screen door at the front and back of the government apartments, and both of my wooden doors were open. The latches did not exactly hold the screen doors closed so we could just push them open. That included Erik, as he would leave whenever he wanted.

The tree was going to go against the window, between our two lounge chairs. I figured we were married and did not need a couch to cuddle on, right? Ok, that is another issue; back to the tree.

I put the tree into a can of dirt, put some water in the can, and tied the tree to the window cranks which opened the windows. There it was; Christmas tree in the house, and cost me nothing. Beth came out and she and I stood about 10 feet from the tree, and thanked me for being "Mr. Man" and bringing in a tree.

Erik must have been asleep in the bedroom because I had not seen him until he came up behind us and stopped. I distinctly remember seeing him stop. Then, as Beth and I were looking at the tree, again, time stood still; Erik walked up to the tree, hoisted his leg, and took about an eight second pee (count it out, it was long) on the middle of the tree.

When Erik was done, he calmly walked to the front door, pushed the door open with his nose, and walked out the door. When the door slammed, I knew Beth would be looking at me. She was. I did the mature thing; I busted out laughing as she began telling me to clean up the carpet.

Erik peed on Christmas. I will never forget the look on Beth's face. It was funny. Yeah it was, we guys laughed, and the guys were in trouble.

Do you remember when your dog did the "leg hoist" at Christmas or other occasions?

Chapter Thirteen: The Vaccination Clinic Fight

Male dogs find female dogs, and are not shy about approaching a female dog. The female dog does not care what kind of car you drive or your family connections. A dog does not need to "feed her a line" to get a female's attention. Many male dogs feel a need, or instinct, to fight off other male dogs if they sense a threat.

Erik quickly learned the law of the jungle. A large German Shepherd named Zeus whipped Erik when Erik "nosed around" a female in whom Zeus had an interest. No big deal; Zeus belonged to my friend Mari, and we laughed at Erik's persistence.

As with most male dogs, when they were not home, there was no telling what they were doing. Below is a story which Erik thought was a secret, but his secret was revealed by another dog, not a human.

One afternoon a pet vaccination clinic was being held in our college town. The meeting place was behind one of the two gasoline stations, named Kennedy's (where Erik met the cop and took the midnight ride). The station across the street was owned by Butch Sain. That will be important in a moment.

There must have been 30 students and locals standing behind Kennedy's on that afternoon waiting to have their dogs and cats vaccinated. Our neighbors, Ray and Anne Callaham, stood in line next to Beth and me. Ray had their cat in his arms. Erik was standing next to me and was not on a leash. Erik was well behaved, but sometimes I had to lean down and grab his collar.

Beth and I were about in the middle of the line facing the rear of Kennedy's gasoline station. The area was grassy, mostly a place for repaired cars to be parked. Beth and I had been in line for maybe 10 minutes, then all hell broke loose. Butch Sain, the owner of the gas station across from Kennedy's, had walked around the corner of the building, and appeared to be walking toward the crowd of people. Butch had two huge German Shepherd's with him, and both were on chain leashes. I looked across the grassy area, about 150 feet, and saw Butch and his dogs. Suddenly, both of Butch's dogs lurched forward and one of the dogs broke the chain leash. The dog, which probably weighed well over 100 pounds, ran full throttle toward the line of pet owners. People scattered, girls squealed, men cursed, and everyone grabbed their pets and ran.

I stood still.

The German Shepherd charged straight toward me, or at Erik, who was a bit over a year old. Butch was running after his dog as he tried to control the other dog who was still on a leash. As the loose dog approached me, I picked up Erik by the neck and collar to the height of my chest. The Shepard leaped into the air and bit Erik in the face. Erik tried to fight but he had no leverage with his feet being off the ground. Erik would not have been a match for that huge dog, but it would have been a fight. Butch caught up to his dog and grabbed him by the collar. The "fight" or "bite" was over. There was not much blood.

Butch started apologizing as the crowd came back into line. "I am so sorry, but your dog is the most persistent dog I have ever seen," said Butch.

Beth was now standing next to me, and since this sounded like Butch was going to tell me an "Erik" story, I figured I was going to be in trouble again. I was.

"You know where I live, up Poverty Hill?"

"Yeah," I said, "that's about a half mile from my apartment."

Butch continued. "About a month ago, my female Shepard was in heat. I put her inside my house and put the two males in the pen behind the house. One morning, I heard my dogs barking, so I looked out the back window and saw your dog come into the back yard. I didn't pay much attention to your dog. I put my female in the house because she was in heat, and your dog must have gotten a whiff of my female."

"My dogs wouldn't stop barking and they got real loud. Your dog was walked over to the dog pen where my two males were barking like hell. My dogs were going crazy, then your dog pissed through the fence onto my dogs. He kicked up some grass and then walked away."

You should have seen the look I got from Beth.

"I went outside and saw that your dog had dug a hole next to my house all the way down to the foundation trying to get to my female. That dog was determined."

"I guess your dog's have a good memory" I told Butch. Erik was not really hurt, scratched a bit. The people returned to the line, slowly. There were two angry Shepard's in line to be vaccinated, but they did not stand next to us.

Dogs recognize other dogs. That is a neat thing to see, but it was not this time.

Do you remember seeing your dog recognizing another dog?

J.B. Simms

Chapter Fourteen: Dog Farts are Still Funny

We men think this is funny; the dog farts and clears the room. Those stories are legendary. This is a bit different, and got me into trouble because I laughed.

Christmas was over. The tree that Erik peed on was now gone. The windows where the tree was placed were uncovered, and faced the street. I could see the college dining hall through this big window, and many times my immature friends (Beth's words) would drive by and yell something obscene. They could see me sitting in my chair through the bit window. There were two smaller crank-out windows on the sides of the big window. Beth and I had separate recliner chairs and no couch. Between our chairs was a lamp stand. It was not very romantic, but hey, I was married. There was no need for cuddling, right?

Around the time for the evening meal, one of my friends drove past my apartment and slowed down to turn left behind the dining hall. They began yelling "Duke, Duke". Erik got up off the floor, put his front paws onto the window sill, and began barking at those idiots. Beth was sitting in her chair, and spun the chair around to be about 4 feet from Erik's back. Her face was about the level of the window sill.

I turned around and saw a passenger in a car "mooning" me; mooning me when I was in my own apartment. How rude. I never knew who it was. Erik continued to bark.

Beth snapped at Erik, "Erik be quiet." Beth was a sweetie, and good to Erik, but sometimes he would just become annoying. Erik enjoyed doing that.

Right after Beth yelled at Erik, as if on cue, with Beth's face probably no further than 3 feet from Erik's back, and her head being a bit below Erik's head, Erik cut the loudest dog fart I ever heard from a dog. (I am laughing as I type. It is still funny). Beth screamed "ERIK! GET DOWN FROM THERE! OH, MY GOD." Erik looked over his right shoulder right into Beth's eyes. He kind of stepped down off the window sill and walked out the screen door, which is what he normally would do if he were in trouble.

The dog farted in Beth's face. I was in trouble again. This dog had no shame.

Do you remember the dog farts?

Yeah, My Dog Did That, Too

Chapter Fifteen: The Graduation Party

This is our college graduation picture, 1975.

The time during graduation from Erskine College was supposed to be fun. Beth graduated with honors, and I had a 2.4 GPA but I told her that I get my diploma 10 seconds after she got her diploma, so it did not matter. When she was irritated with me, she would call me "2.4" and my opinion drifted away.

The president, Dr. Wightman, was hosting a steak cookout, having the graduating seniors at his house in his large back yard. Large tables, picnic style, were scattered across the lawn. Men brought us steaks and it was nice.

Dr. Wightman had a dachshund, you know, the weenie dog. The dog was walking around the back yard and people were petting the dog. The dog could smell a hundred or more steaks being cooked and people were cutting fat off the steaks and feeding the weenie dog.

Someone sitting next to me said, "Erik's here." There he was; he found me. He had to have smelled the meat being cooked, and I just happened to be there. I did not need to be "there" for Erik to show up, anywhere.

I called him over to me. The people at the table began giving him scraps and he was easy to feed. He was playing "nice dog" and played to the crowd.

Dr. Wightman's dog walked up about 15 feet from me, and stood next to Erik. It was as though Erik was bigger and the weenie dog wanted to be with the big dog. It was ok for a minute, but when that weenie dog jumped for a meat scrap in front of Erik, Erik turned like a snake and bit the weenie dog and latched on. The dog squealed like hell. Everyone was watching. I got the President's dog out of Erik's mouth as the President's wife came over to rescue that little wiener dog. Why that dog came over where Erik was sitting I never know, but I was in trouble again.

Do you remember when your dog was in public, and there was seemingly a tranquil situation, until food became an issue?

Do you remember when your dog appeared unannounced, and uninvited, to a social gathering?

Chapter Sixteen: Not Sharing the Car Seat

Have you ever had the dog who would not move after he/she got comfortable? The most irritating "Erik in the car story" was just after my college graduation. I had learned that an uncle had been in a bad automobile accident and Beth and I had to go to Florida. We picked up my cousin 30 miles away and began the all-night trek to Tampa. Beth and Erik were in the back seat. Although the back seat of a Mustang was small, it was big enough for Beth (a bit over 5 feet tall, weighing less than 110 pounds) and a dog.

My cousin was asleep in the passenger seat. He was 11 years older than me and I was hoping he could help drive. After he drove for about 20 minutes, I saw his head bobbing, and I decided to take over driving. For some reason, I either looked toward the back or Beth said something to me and I saw that Beth had her head on the seat, but she was not sitting on the seat; she was sitting on the floor. I asked her what she was doing on the floor. She looked at me and said, "Erik won't move."

I felt terrible. Erik had sprawled his ass across the entire seat and Beth either could not move him (he probably weighed 75 pounds) or she might have been afraid to move him.

That did not last long. I yelled so loudly at Erik that he was startled, as were the others in the car. Erik knew exactly why I was yelling at him. The words "get down" were probably in his vocabulary by that time, and he knew by the tone of my voice that he had better do something fast. He moved off the seat onto the floor so Beth was able to sit on the back seat.

The dog thought he could sit anywhere he wanted.

You have chased your dog off a couch, chair, or bed so you can sit. He will not move unless you make him move, or you stare him down. It is funny when you think you can stare down your dog, and the dog does not move.

Do you remember the look your dog gave you when you told him to move to another seat in the car?

Chapter Seventeen: These Chewed Shoes Don't Match

A few weeks after graduation, I got a job in Columbia, SC. Beth and I had never lived in Columbia, so this was an adventure for a newly married couple, new college graduates, and the dog.

I had a job waiting on me, and Beth took a part time job at a department store before she got a job teaching school. Being gone all day was different than going to school and being around from time to time, so guess who had to adjust, the dog, Erik.

Erik had never been cooped up in an apartment all day. In the mornings, I would open the sliding glass door at the rear of the apartment and simply let him go outside. He always returned before Beth and I had to go to work, which was about an hour or so. I would leave the sliding door open a bit and he would appear a brief time later. One time I could see that he had been in a fight because he had blood on one of his ears. I did not see a cut, so I figured the blood did not belong to Erik. Leash laws were not enforced often in 1975, or I just ignored them.

You must remember having to keep your dog in an apartment all day, worrying about the dog messing up something or pooping or whatever, especially a puppy. Erik was no puppy, probably a year and a half old, but he still had to stay in an apartment all day for the first time.

At the time, Beth and I had one car when we moved to Columbia, so I picked her up after her work-day ended. Luckily, she was working downtown, which was near my job. When we got home one day, Beth went into the apartment ahead of me. I heard Beth call of the dog's name, "ERIK!!!" That did not sound good.

Beth walked out of the bedroom with two shoes. "Erik chewed up my shoes." It was not funny, but when you are 21 years old and the dog ate your wife's shoe, it was funny.

I looked at the shoes, and to my horror, the shoes did not match. I was in a world of hurt now.

Ok, guys, I know you remember when the dog ate the wife's shoes, or something else in the house, and what the dog ate belonged to the wife?

Chapter Eighteen: Beth Goes Flying

Erik had learned to "go hide" which meant "get under the bed and stay there until I tell you that you can come out." Well, it he became comfortable under the bed and slept under the bed many times.

On this night, a month or so after we had settled into our new apartment, I was lying on my back, fast asleep, with Beth lying to my right. No one was touching each other, and after you read this story you will see it would be a while before we touched again.

As I lay there, face up, the bed slats on my side of the bed collapsed. The box springs hit the floor, with the mattress and me, and Beth, on top of the mattress. I sprung off that bed so fast it was unbelievable. I spun around and faced the side of the bed, thinking Erik was under the collapsed bed. I reached under the box spring and the bed rail, and flipped the entire bed over against the wall on the side where Beth was sleeping. The bed was probably four feet from the wall on Beth's side.

Here is the picture; the bed on Beth's side was about 4 feet from the wall. When I grabbed the box spring, with mattress, and Beth on top of the mattress, I flipped everything over against the wall on Beth's side of the bed. The entire bed, minus the frame, rotated toward the wall, and the box spring was leaning against the wall at about a 45-degree angle. The mattress and Beth, were on top of the box spring as Beth slept, but were now both upside down and leaning against the wall.

I looked on the floor, thinking Erik had been under there. He was not. In my horror, I turned and ran toward one of the two bathrooms in the hallway. I turned on the light and there he was, lying on the cool tile floor.

The sound of me flipping the bed into the air woke him, but when I turned on the light, I saw that he was awake, and looked annoyed that I woke him. I was so glad he was not under the bed; it would have crushed him.

I had to go back into the bedroom. The bed was still leaning against the wall. Beth appeared; walking out from under the triangle shaped area made by the leaning bed. What I did not realize when I flipped the bed into the air was that poor Beth was launched into the air and onto the floor, straight from a dead sleep. (I am laughing over 40 years later). She looked at me as the fool I was. My laughing did not help much.

I fixed the slats on the rails, and put the bed back down. Beth got back into the bed. My apology did not mean much because I could not stop laughing. Erik heard Beth talking, but the tone of her voice made Erik stay in the bathroom. There was no snuggling.

Have you ever thrown your wife out of bed, thinking that the bed collapsed on the dog?

Chapter Nineteen: New Neighborhood: New Dog Fight

In late October of 1975, we moved out of the apartment to a house that had a back yard. Erik could be in the back yard and not eat the inside of the house.

On the first weekend after moving, the weather had cooled off a bit. I was cutting weeds and vines off a wire fence (normally called a welded wire or two-by-four wire fence) and the bushes were thick as hell. Erik was in the back yard with me. A man living in the house across this fence came up to speak to me. I remember his name was Bill; he was a car salesman, and a very nice man. He was probably in his 50's.

We talked probably 10 minutes or so and I could see he had a dog, a mutt, like Erik, and the dog came up to the fence. I could not get close enough to the dog to pet him or have him lick my hand because the growth of bushes, vines, thorns, and a few wild thorny rose bushes, kept me at a bit of a distance.

Here came trouble. When Bill's dog came up, Erik walked over. The dogs were probably 6 to 8 feet apart, and you could tell this was not going to be good. The dogs started the growling thing and Bill and I both exchanged what nice dogs the other had.

I tried to get Erik to stop growling and barking at Bill's dog, and Bill was doing the same with his dog. Bill's side of the fence was clear; the thorns and vines were on my side. The bushes were thorny and I had a problem getting to Erik as he went face to face with Bill's dog through the fence. Bill's dog realized how flimsy the fence was and came over the fence in to my yard. Both dogs started a fight and the bushes and thorns did not stop the dogs. The dogs were about the same size, and Bill's dog was a bit older.

Bill and I struggled to up those testosterone-driven dogs in the thorns of wild vines and rose bushes.

It was a good thing it was not our wives who witnessed these two male dogs fighting. I am not being sexist, but there was no time to hesitate. Bill had climbed over the fence and both he and I were tangled up in the bushes as we grabbed our dogs.

Do you remember moving to a new neighborhood and having dogs "mark their territory" to let the other dogs know who has moved in?

Chapter Twenty: Call the Food Police

The dog fight previously mentioned had ended. Neither dog was hurt, but two dogs fighting is a nasty sound, especially when neither is giving up.

Erik was basking in the sun after his fight with Bill's dog as I continued to clean out brush from the back yard of the new rental house. Beth was in the house unpacking from our move from the apartment.

I believe it was Halloween night when we moved into the new house, in Columbia, South Carolina and the weather was still hot. Beth brought out drinks and then, as the caring young wife (she did well) she brought out sandwiches for us to eat in the back yard. I sat on the concrete porch as she brought out the paper plates full of food. Erik walked up the steps as I was sitting with my legs hanging off the porch. Beth handed me my plate, put her plate down, and went back inside for something.

I looked to my left and Erik snapped up Beth's sandwich off the plate and took it into the yard. He acted as though he assumed the plate was his food she brought for him. He turned around to face me from about 30 feet away. It was like watching a frog catch a fly; he took her food so quickly I could not speak. I knew I was in big, big trouble.

Beth walked out and said, "Where's my sandwich?" She looked out into the yard and Erik was looking at her as he ate her sandwich. My mouth was full. I tried not to laugh, but I am sure I did.

About a month or so later I was sitting in the living room watching television. We ate off TV trays much of the time.

Again, Beth brought out plates of food and put the plates on the small folding TV trays we placed in front of the couch so we could eat and watch television. Erik watched an animal on a show called Wild Kingdom and barked at the television. Beth laughed at Erik, and went back into the kitchen. I was not paying much attention to Erik, and then Erik walked in front of me. He quickly took a piece of meat off Beth's plate, and walked into another room to eat. I could see him eating it and knew I was again in big, big, big, trouble. I had no idea the dog was waiting for her to put down the food and leave.

Again, Beth returned, my mouth was full, as was Erik's.

That was the last time he did that. He did that twice within a week. I knew that if I were to have any children with Beth, I would have to stop Erik from taking her food.

Do you remember when you put down your food and the dog took your food off your plate?

Chapter Twenty-One: Just Drop the Leash

Even after Erik had twice taken food off Beth's plate, she still loved the dog. Well, I was the one who got into trouble and suffered the consequences, and I believe he knew that. I was accused of encouraging him in his mischief. I did, sometimes, and it was fun to do. Beth's reactions to this dog's mischief was priceless.

One evening Beth and I decided to walk around the neighborhood. We had gotten a dog from the pound to be with Erik, a terrier type named Taffy, so the four of us did the walk thing. Beth had Taffy on the leash and I had Erik. Beth was walking on my right.

We walked down a street which was parallel to our house, and behind our house. As we walked I looked down the street and since we were walking on the left side of the street, I could see a dog that looked like a boxer on the front porch of a house about 4 houses away. The house was on the right side of the road.

Suddenly, the dog bolted off the front porch and headed straight toward us. Taffy ran in front of me, under Erik's leash. Beth went behind me, so my feet were tied together. I was screwed but the funny part was Beth had no idea what she had done.

I did the best thing; I dropped the leash and Erik and the boxer looked like they hit head on in the middle of the street. Erik was about 2 years old, and he had his butt whipped by a big German Shepherd, so he learned how to fight. Those dogs made such a commotion. That is always a nasty sound when dogs fight.

Erik evidently got the upper hand (or paw) and chased the boxer to the house where I first saw him. The boxer stopped and they began again for a minute, then Erik walked back to us as I tried to untangle my feet.

He was out of the doghouse for taking Beth's food. All she could do was shake her head. She was not crazy about the dog fight thing, but she had to have been glad he was there. All the transgressions seemed to have been forgiven, but there were more transgressions to come.

Do you remember when your dog protected you without you having to say anything?

Chapter Twenty-Two: A Fence Is No Barrier

After living in the small house for about 8 months, we bought a house.

Our new dog, Taffy, was there to keep Erik occupied, and maybe keep him home. That did not work out so well.

We bought a chain link fence for the back yard, probably spent a thousand dollars. This was the first fence erected at the back of the property, only because we had DOGS, and you know how we are about DOGS, so we spent the money.

Remember trying to secure the fence in the back yard? Remember the holes your dog dug to get out? Well, Erik was Houdini. That dog must have laid down next to the fence and crawled upside down to get out. I never understood how a dog could get out in so many places.

The man across the street had a bunch of tin. I cut the lengths in half, lengthwise, and buried the tin at the base of the chain link fence, between the posts. I punched holes in the top of the tin and attached the fence with wire. The damned dog broke the tie wires. I tied fencing to the top of a fence, in a corner, to keep Erik from using a corner of the fence for leverage. Erik butted his head against the horizontal wire on the five-foot chain link fence until he broke the tie wires above him. He crawled out between the horizontal fencing and the corner post, balanced himself, and jumped off the top of the fence to freedom.

After I thought I had secured the area under the fence, Erik began jumping up, attaching himself to the top of the fence in areas other than the corners, and leaping off the five-foot tall fence.

My close friend from college, Tom Burdyl, lived nearby. Tom knew Erik when I first got Erik because although Tom had graduated, he returned to visit friends on many weekends and he and Erik shared either a chair or the couch in my apartment with Bernie Vitti.

I told Tom that Erik was getting up over the 5-foot fence. He did not believe me. One day Tom was at my house and I proved it. I put Erik in the back yard and Tom and I watched from the den window. Erik walked across the yard and looked around as if to see if the coast was clear. He walked to a corner of the fence and stood as close as he could and jumped straight up. His front feet landed on the opposite side of the fence, and his back feet were about a foot on the other side. He got his balance and leaped off the top of the fence like a cat, and he was gone.

Tom remembers that to this day.

Do you remember the fence you built to keep the dog the yard? Remember the pain it was trying to find out where the dog was getting out? Remember seeing your dog on your front porch when you got home?

Chapter Twenty-Three: The Pecking Order

Brian Burdyl with his dogs, Orbit and Pluto.
Orbit (the older (left), mother) and Pluto were long- time friends with Erik.

My friend, Tom Burdyl, would return to school to visit from time to time. He had graduated before me. Tom needed a place to "crash" so he always ended up at the apartment where Bernie and I lived. Since the door was never locked, Tom could come in anytime and sleep on the couch, or in the big green lounge chair. Tom became my closest friend, spanning over 40 years.

Tom was good to Erik. I would awaken to find Tom either on the couch or in the lounge chair, asleep, and Erik asleep on the furniture which Tom abandoned. If Tom was in the chair, it meant that Erik had commandeered the couch and Tom was not going to move the dog.

Do you remember how your good friends deferred to the dog when it came to spots to sit or sleep? Dogs ruled the house.

Years later, Tom and I lived in Columbia, SC. Tom and his wife, Laurette, had springer spaniels. Tom would bring Orbit and Pluto to my house and put them in the back yard with Erik. Pluto was in the yard and squatted to pee. Erik came along and raised his leg and pee on top of where Pluto peed. Pluto was a male, but had never been around another grown male dog, and had never seen a dog raise his leg to pee. Pluto learned that day. Tom and I watched and laughed.

Pluto learned another lesson; never eat from the food bowl of another dog. Pluto was young, and he was raised by his mother, Orbit, so Pluto had not been around many dogs other than his mother. When Pluto was at my house, he walked over to Erik's bowl (it was outside) and Erik calmly walked over, grabbed Pluto by the back of the neck, and slung him to the ground. Orbit stood by, casually watching her son learn a lesson from an older male dog. Lesson learned. They all became good friends, and although Pluto was a tough dog himself, the respect he always showed Erik was evident. Orbit, Pluto's mother, did not defend Pluto when Erik jumped on Pluto. Orbit and Erik had been around each other for years, and Orbit knew that Pluto was learning a lesson.

All our dogs protect their domain. Some give allowances to dogs who are not a threat (like Orbit) but this was a good lesson for Pluto. Pluto then protected his domain. There are more domain stories to follow.

Do you remember seeing your dog protecting his domain and establishing the dog pecking order in a group of dogs?

Chapter Twenty-Four: Neighbors Knew Your Dog First

Erik gets a bath from Joe. I cannot tell whose face is funnier.
Kids love to bathe the dog, but parents are nearby with towels when the dog jumps out.

When Beth and I bought our first house (1976), I was working for a finance company, Household Finance. For those of you who never heard the words "finance company," these were lending businesses for persons who might not have a high credit score, or just needed a small amount of money. I took applications, made loans, and chased those who would not pay. Beth had gotten a job teaching school. The office where I worked was only fewer than 2 miles from my house, so this was beautiful for me. We found out fast that we did not own Erik; we shared him.

I learned how to close loans at 22 years of age, and there was a bit of responsibility closing a loan by yourself at a closing table. I am sure customers wondered about our age, but we had good teachers.

One day I had to close a loan and I looked at the loan packet. I noticed the address of the lady borrowing the money, and realized she lived about 3 houses from my house. She came into the office and sat at the second of 3 tables. Her son was with her and I recognized her son. I had lived in the neighborhood for a couple of months, and did know the names of some of the kids. I did know this kid was Tommy Hogue. Tommy was probably about 10 years old. I was surprised to see young Tommy with his mother.

I took the packet to the table and sat across from Ms. Hogue.

"Hi Tommy," I said, "and good afternoon Ms. Hogue. I am Jim Simms. I live in the house on the corner of Plumer and Springhill, right down the street from your house. I see Tommy out all the time."

Tommy piped up, "Yeah mom, he is Erik's daddy."

I knew Erik was making the rounds in the neighborhood. I had never had a conversation with Tommy, just knowing his name to speak. How did he know Erik's name? Did Erik tell him? Sounds like Erik had been making the rounds.

Did your neighbors know the name of your dog before they knew your name?

Chapter Twenty-Five: Recognizing a "Doggie Bag"

Erik always ate scraps along with dog food. I guess he got used to doing that by eating out of the kitchen garbage can. Some dogs can eat anything, and some have such sensitive digestive systems that they can only eat specific foods. Erik was a goat-dog; he could eat anything. I would put scraps from my plate into his bowl (what I did not feed him from the table). One time I put the leftovers of a salad into his bowl. He ate everything except for the cucumbers.

When we first moved to our house, we would go out to eat with our friends, and where do young people go out to eat? They eat pizza.

There was always pizza left to take home, but coming into the house with a take-out pizza box was dangerous. You had to get past Erik to get to the refrigerator. He always got a couple of pieces until it got to be a habit just to come into the house and split the pizza between Erik and Taffy. There was never any leftover pizza to put into the refrigerator, and we knew not to come home empty handed.

Do you remember having to feed your dog pizza? Do you remember the look the dog gave you until you gave him the pizza?

Chapter Twenty-Six: An Amazing Instinct

Remember the story about Erik going to Butch Sain's house when I was in college and enraging the German Shepherd dogs as he tried to get to the dog which was in heat? That scent is supposed to travel up to a mile, and Erik had a bionic nose.

One night, soon after moving into our house (1976) and having put up the fence (at least it looked nice and Taffy never got out), I walked into the back yard and Erik went with me. Our yard/lot had some heavily wooded areas and a dog could easily hide back there. This night Erik casually walked away from me, walked directly to the back corner of the property, and jumped the fence. I yelled at him but that was worthless.

I came back into the house and told Beth that Erik was gone again. I got into my car and drove 2 blocks to a heavily traveled road which was in the middle of the neighborhood. I turned to the right, drove up the hill about a quarter of mile, looked to my left, and there he was, fighting a dog in someone's front yard. I parked my car in the driveway as the dog Erik was fighting scampered away. Erik looked at me as if to say, "I am the man" but he knew he was in trouble for getting out. Erik looked at me, then walked over to the front porch where a young man was standing with a small white dog.

As I got out of my car I saw a young man, about my age, on the front porch. I said to the man, "Man, I am sorry. He jumped the fence and ..."

"Don't worry, it is alright. By the way, do you want to mate your dog with mine? She is in heat. Her name is Sugar."

Erik looked at me as though he understood the man. Erik had to think it was funny that the owner of this white dog wanted Erik to mate with his dog. Dogs can tell by the tone of our voices that the conversation is friendly, and Erik knew he had escaped punishment.

I swear Erik winked at me when the guy asked if it would be alright if Erik mated with his dog. I guess he felt he earned the right because he had defended the honor of the white dog. Yeah, right; defended her honor.

"Well, I guess my dog would not mind. You want to follow me to my house? It is right around the block." Erik was very happy, and eaten up with anxiety. A dog in heat in the back yard, a yard with a fence. Erik would have access to Sugar, 24/7. She can't get out.

I told the guy where I lived and he was going to come by later. It was already about 8pm by the time I left.

The guy arrived at my house about 20 minutes after I got home. We went to one of the gates and put Sugar into the back yard. Erik was in the back yard. Taffy was in the backyard too, but Erik was not paying any attention to Taffy.

Yes, Erik was in heaven.

One afternoon a few days later, the 9- year old girl named Catherine, who live next door, walked over to our house. She had a friend with her, another little girl. Catherine had been to our house many times and knew Taffy and Erik.

As she and her friend walked to the fence near my garage, Beth was standing at the window watching the girls. Catherine said to her friend, "That's Taffy, and that's Sugar, and that's Erik on top of Sugar." Beth could not wait to tell me about Erik mounting Sugar in front of two young girls, and hear what Catherine had said. Beth was so embarrassed. I could not wait to tell Catherine's parents, Jack and Sue.

After a week or so, Sugar went home. Erik was one tired dog.

The gestation period for a dog is 63 days, or 7 weeks, so the ending of this story evidently occurred about 2 months after Erik's week in heaven.

A few months after Erik's "honeymoon" on a Friday afternoon, I drove home after work into my driveway and parked in front of the closed garage door. There he was, Erik, sitting on the retaining wall to my right. He was not behind the fence, he was free and I had no idea how he got out or if Beth let him out. The odd thing was that he was sitting on the wall seemingly waiting for me to come home. I got out of my car and Erik jumped down from the wall and trotted down the street away from me. I called to him, nicely, and then I yelled at him. He looked back at me then continued to trot away from me. Yes, he stopped in the street to look back at me. Well, I thought if I followed him I would eventually be able to grab him, but I did not know where I was going.

I followed him from about 100 feet behind him. He walked two blocks, and then turned right and walked on the sidewalk next to a busy two-lane road. I turned right, going up the hill on the sidewalk, and Erik was still up ahead of me.

About 100 yards up the hill Erik stopped and crossed the street to his left. I remembered that was where Sugar lived. I wondered why he was leading me to this house.

I crossed the street as Erik walked to the right side of the house and out of view. As I got to the back of the house I found Erik sitting at the bottom of about 15 concrete steps leading to a landing at the back door. On the landing was a cardboard box. I could see Sugar was sitting next to the box. Erik walked half way up the steps and Sugar snarled at him. I walked up, stood next to Erik, and saw what was in the box; a bunch of Erik and Sugar puppies. I did not go too close to Sugar, only her owner would be able to do that. Evidently, Erik brought me to see his kids.

Later in the evening, I contacted Sugar's owner. He was amazed that Erik led me to see his parents. I ended up getting a couple of the puppies, taking a few to a pet store and one to one of my coworkers.

The communication between Erik and me was spooky. Erik knew he was taking me to see his puppies. That was too weird.

Do you remember when your dog did something which made you think there was some weird kind of communication between you and your dog?

Chapter Twenty-Seven: Protecting the Neighbor's House

Salem (larger) and Camas, belonged to Walt and Mary Ann Smith.
They were beautiful dogs, and friends of Erik.
They lived across the street, and next door to the Middlebrooks.

Erik roamed the neighborhood. Many people in the neighborhood fed him treats and actual food when he came over. He played with all the kids. Most of the neighborhood dogs were his friend (there were a few fights with other dogs) as well as the humans. Salem and Camas were beautiful Goldens who lived across the street.

He was friendly with the grown-ups as well as the kids. Sometimes I figured that the adults just tolerated dogs, but this was a fitting story of a neighbor lady turning from tolerating Erik to being grateful.

One couple who lived across the street from our house was Tommy and Brandy Middlebrooks. They were great people. Tommy was a high school football star who hurt his knee in college, and Brandy, well Brandy was the prettiest female (next to our wives of course) in the neighborhood. Brandy was gorgeous, and tough as nails. She was easy to kid with, and she could give it back just as well. Tommy was the same age as Beth and me, Brandy a year younger. We were in our early twenties and none of us had kids, so pets were the kids at that time. Tommy and Brandy lived next to Walt and Mary Ann.

Erik had been to every house within a few blocks of his home. Since the five-foot fence would not hold him, he would show up at someone's house, and the owners would feed him snacks as he just hung around. If a grill was fired up, he would be there.

Sometimes he would sleep on a neighbor's porch for shade, out of the sun. He wanted a cool place to sleep.

During any day, you would find Erik snoozing on the front porch of anyone's house. You might ask why he was not in my house or in my back yard. If he were in the back yard, the fence was simply a decoration to him, and there were times he would just want to go out and wander. There was never a worry; he would come home when he wanted.

Brandy had an edge about her, as if she knew everything we were thinking, and she did. Brandy, Beth, and Mary Ann, along with the other ladies, made great friends. Brandy was well acquainted with Erik, and had taken Erik with her and her daughter and Joey as they collected candy during Halloween. There is a photo of the kids, in their costumes, and Erik. I wish I could find that picture.

One Saturday morning I was over at Tommy and Brandy's house to help Tommy do something. Erik was with me. I knocked on the door and Brandy answered the door.

"Good morning Erik. Come on in." Brandy turned and led Erik into the house, then turned around to me, front door still open, and said, " Good morning Jim. You can come in too." That was Brandy being funny.

Bandy called Erik into the kitchen and gave him food from the refrigerator. That was usual for me to do, but seeing Brandy do that floored me, until she told me this story.

Brandy said, "Jim, a couple of days ago, I got a call from Hal (Middlebrooks, Tommy's dad) and Hal told me he came by the house and there was a dog asleep at the front door. Hal said he got out of his car to knock on the door and the dog growled at him and would not let him near the house. Hal comes over here unannounced all the time, and I wish he would quit that, and he did it again. This time Erik was on the porch, and Hal told me he got into his car and left. From now on, Erik can sleep at our door anytime, he is always welcome, and he gets what he wants from my fridge."

This was hilarious. Brandy was always a bit like the neighborhood diva, and territorial. She hated unannounced "drop-ins". It invaded her privacy. Now Erik was the hero, and Tommy's dad needed a reservation before coming over next time.

Erik earned refrigerator food again.

Do you remember your surprise at the relationship your dog had with other humans?

Chapter Twenty-Eight: Dogs Learn to Open Doors

Dogs are smart. We all know that. They watch us when we don't expect it. They learn from us.

One day I was arriving home and there was a crowd in my front yard. I got out of the car and walked up to Beth. She told me a lady was walking a dachshund in front of our house (the dog was on a leash) and Erik started barking at the dog from inside our front door. Beth was not concerned, just tried to get Erik to shut up.

Suddenly, Erik jumped up on his back legs, put a front paw on the latch of the storm door, and opened the door. His weight pushed the door open enough for him to escape, and he bolted across the yard, grabbing the dachshund by the head, a tug of war began between the lady and Erik. The screaming was so intense that a neighbor named Tom Brantley, from 4 houses away, ran to my house. Evidently the lady did not see Tom arrive from down the street, because Tom told me the lady gave Tom a royal cussing out. She thought Tom was married to Beth.

Erik was in trouble. Erik thought he was defending his territory, and that the dog was in our (his) yard, we had to pay for the dog's veterinarian bill. Then she said she was going to sue us. That did not happen, but we kept the door a bit more secure.

 We got that door fixed.

Do you remember when the dog opened the door to the house to go after another dog?

Yeah, My Dog Did That, Too

Chapter Twenty-Nine: Calculated Revenge

Joe is using Erik for balance as Joe learned to walk, holding onto Erik's fur.
He left his bottle in the middle of the floor to play with Erik.
That "beak" you see in the upper right corner is mine.

I know there must have been some vicarious jealousy between Erik and me. I was jealous that he could sleep all day, eat, roam the neighborhood, and chase female dogs when they were in heat. This dog was the most prolific female chaser I had ever seen; not just chasing females, but fighting for them and getting to them. He had to be jealous because I could drive a car and I was still the boss.

A few months before Joe was born, I took a job with a bank located about 70 miles from Columbia. The town was Pageland, SC. There were two traffic lights, a sandwich shop, two banks, and about 4 churches.

We bought a house which was situated right across an unmarked blacktop road from a softball field. I loved it because during the spring and summer, I could walk across the street to play. I did not erect a fence, so the dogs ran free.

One Saturday, Beth reminded me that Erik had been gone all night, and was not home. Beth like the dogs more than she ever admitted. Erik was like the 13-year old kid; Beth was amused and annoyed, but loved him. So, I looked around (that was a waste of time, and I knew it) then got into my car to look for him.

I left the driveway and headed east for less than a block, and turned north. I really had no idea where I was going, but something led me in this direction. After about a mile, a turn was made onto a dirt road which I had never seen. About 200 feet down the road was a concrete block house. The area in front of the porch was all dirt; it was where people parked their cars. This was a very rural area.

As I looked to my left upon approaching the house, I first saw the house, then the two-step porch. On top of the porch was a dog; medium sized, and looked like it was asleep. Lying on the step below the top of the porch was Erik, king of his domain. In the dirt driveway/parking area were two dogs, lying in the dirt about 100 feet from the porch. It was a standoff; Erik had conquered the area and now the female was his.

I drove into the dirt, but not close enough to disturb the two dogs. Erik saw me drive up. I got out of my car, stood between the open car door and the car itself, looked at him and said, "Stay there, it is ok." Our eyes met. We both understood that if I called him to me, the fight would be two on one. It was not that he could not take care of himself, but we both knew the game. I got back into the car and drove back to my house. I told Beth what happened and she was ok with that.

About two hours later, Erik showed up. He was fed, drank water, and left again. He needed some nourishment; he was a busy boy.

The next morning, Erik returned. He was injured. His front right leg had been bitten, near the paw. Damn it, Erik. I took bandages I had used for myself sliding as I played softball (I was 25 years old, most of us would slide back then) and wrapped his foot. He could barely put his foot on the floor. He stayed in the house sleeping a lot after that.

The following Monday I came home for lunch. The bank was close by, there was no traffic, Joey was an infant, and we had a babysitter named Monica. Beth was teaching school. I fixed my food, placed it on a TV table and sat on the couch watching television. The front door was open, exposing the screen door. Erik was sleeping on the concrete porch.

I happened to look out across my yard toward the softball field and to my amazement; one of the two dogs I saw in the dirt driveway on Saturday was across the street, using my yard to cut across toward an unknown destination. Erik saw him; I knew it because even though Erik was lying down, I saw his ears poke up. He remained very still. I softly called Monica over to watch because I knew what was going to happen.

The dog blindly walked across my front yard, about 20 yards from my front porch. He did not see Erik lying on the porch. What a dumb dog.

In an instant, Erik bolted off the porch heading straight for the dog. The dog froze as Erik ran on three legs. Erik hit, and I mean "hit" the dog with his chest (I know some of you have seen this happen) then grabbed the dog by the neck. Erik had recognized the dog as one of the two who had to have jumped him. He beat that dog soundly, then the dog escaped, and ran. Erik returned to the porch. I opened the screen door, invited him in, patted him on the head, made sure he was not hurt or his foot re-injured, and he jumped up on the couch with Monica to go back to sleep.

Do you remember seeing your dog recognize another dog, especially a foe?

Yeah, My Dog Did That, Too

Chapter Thirty: Erik as the Cookie Monster

Erik, Joe (left), cousin Sam Pettit, Jamie Walker, and John Walker (front right).
Erik was John's "Cookie Monster"

This is where the cute trick turns into disaster.

Erik had learned that it was permissible to take food out of my mouth. He never bit me, was very gentle, but he had to know that Beth did not condone this. It was part of the bond, just dog stuff.

Joey had just been born, and was a few months old. A cousin of mine, named Pam, lived in Charlotte, NC, about 40 miles north of where we were living. Pam planned to come visit and see LBJ (Little Baby Joey) and was coming down on a Friday afternoon. Pam's son, John, was coming with her. John was a year and a half of age.

I was working at the bank, and after work I came home. Pam's car was in the driveway next to my other Mustang (yes, I had two Mustangs). As I pulled into the driveway, Beth was opening the front door of the house and pushing Erik out the front door. I could tell Erik was angry. Taffy, our other dog, and smaller than Erik, followed Erik. After Erik had descended the steps, Taffy ran to Erik, and Erik bit Taffy. All this is happening before I can get out of the car.

I got out of the car, chastised Erik, comforted Taffy, and asked Beth what was going on. By that time, Pam was in the doorway holding her son John. John was crying. Pam said, "Erik bit John" and they went back into the house. I knew that would never have happened so I had to get to the bottom of this.

Here is what happened: While Beth and Pam were doing the goo-goo thing over infant Joey, little John wandered into the bedroom. Of course, Erik was asleep under the bed. John was carrying a cookie in his hand. As he wandered into the bedroom, Erik heard John's tiny steps and began wagging his tail as he lay under the bed. John heard the tail wagging, the tail hitting the floor, so John waddled over to the far edge of the bed to find what was making the thumping sound.

John was, and is a smart kid (he is now a lawyer), so he did not want to lose his cookie as he inspected the unidentified sound. John put the cookie into his mouth, dropped to his knees, and lifted the dust ruffle of the bed. As John lifted the dust ruffle, he stuck his head under the bed where Erik was lying, only a foot or so from John. Remember, the cookie is still in John's mouth and John had no idea what was making that sound.

When John leaned under the bed, Erik leaned forward and took the cookie out of John's mouth. All John saw was a huge dog head (a cookie monster) with huge white teeth going for his face and taking the cookie. John screamed, and Pam came running. Erik had emerged from under the bed and was observed eating John's cookie. Beth was in no position to defend the dog, so she through both dogs out of the house.

The funny part would have been the look on John's face when the dog monster to the cookie, with his mouth, out of John's mouth. Pam and I still refer to this incident to this day.

Did your dog ever unexpectedly, or purposely, take food from someone's mouth?

Chapter Thirty-One: The Dog Pound and the Bank

After moving back to Columbia, we moved back into the house in which we previously lived. Erik was back in the old neighborhood. There was an incident in which he had to re-establish his territory, but I will get to that story a bit later.

Beth had been aggravated with Erik's roaming. There was the incident where the lady showed up at the house one Saturday afternoon, telling Beth that Erik has impregnated her dog just an hour or so ago. She found out who he was, and who we were, came to the house, and claimed Erik had jumped her fence and "gotten to" her female dog. Beth looked at Erik; he just looked away. Beth gave the lady some money for a shot her dog was to get from the veterinarian, gave the lady some churned ice cream which Beth was making for a party that night, and the lady left. Erik then went under the bed, and I was told of the lady's visit when I got home.

About 3 months after we returned to the neighborhood, Erik was missing again. As aggravated as Beth seemed, she put an advertisement in the local newspaper. Beth was in denial about her love for the dog, but he deserved her disdain.

The day the advertisement was published, the dogcatcher called the house. Beth got the call, and the dogcatcher told Beth that he picked had Erik up about 4 blocks from our house. Erik had been in the back yard with a female Doberman, after having scaled a 5-foot fence. The owner of the Doberman told the dog catcher that Erik was very friendly, but she had to tie him to the frame of an oil drum platform to keep him from doing his thing, again. The dogcatcher told Beth that Erik was at the dog pound. Great, I am working at the bank, at a new position, and I should go to the dog pound during my work-day?

I had to plan a secret trip. I took the bank car, a full-sized Chevrolet, so the bank thought I was out on official business. After I got to the office of the dog pound, the clerk told me to walk down the row of cages and see if I could find my dog. As I walked down the aisle, all the dogs started barking. I got near the end of one of the rows, and after being alerted by the barking of all the dogs, all the dogs were looking at me. To my left I see him; Erik was looking to his right, waiting to see who was coming down the aisle. When he saw my face, he was relieved. The acknowledgment was mutual relief, but he knew he was in trouble.

I went back to the desk and had to pay $50.00 to get him out. Damn it. After I got him out, I realized they had sprayed him with some God-awful spray. Into the bank car he jumped, but I did not have time to take him home, so to the bank we went.

My office was on a major street, but the entrance to my office was not the main entrance of the building. I parked in a loading zone, opened the back door, and Erik jumped out, and then ran into the building as I held the door open. I then called him into my office where he slept for the rest of the day.

One of the secretaries from another part of the bank came into my office and sat across from me. Erik's tail began thumping under my desk. She did not tell anyone, but the other people in my office knew he was there.

Going to the dog pound generated many emotions; anger, irritation, joy, and a little laughter when you looked your dog in the eye. You knew your dog wanted to tell you about the dogcatcher.

Did you have you had to go to the pound to get your dog?

Yeah, My Dog Did That, Too

Chapter Thirty-Two: The Protection Game

Erik is kissing Joe. Beth cringed, but understood.
Kids need dog lips.

Dogs seem to understand playing games. I had made a game of taunting Erik when Joe was near Erik, or act menacing toward Joe. This would make Erik bear his teeth and growl at me so intensely that his entire canine teeth could be seen. This was the protection game; Erik was protecting Joe.

We carried the game to the front yard. Joe was about 5 years old, making Erik 10 years old. Joe would run with a football toward me and I would look like I was tackling him. Joe would squeal (kind of embarrassing now, but yes, little Joe squealed) and call for Erik to help, and Erik would come to the rescue.

When Joe would run, I would run toward him, and Erik would get between Joe and me, barking and growling. Joe would run and Erik would not allow me to get to Joe. Erik was running interference.

The game changed when I took the ball. I ran slowly toward Joe, enabling him to "wrap up" my legs, pinning my knees together. (This was early football tackling training). Erik sensed Joe was attacking me, so Erik would bite my pants leg or jump to grab my shirt sleeve. Eventually I would stop and fall to the ground. Joe would laugh in victory; Erik would stand next to Joe, knowing he did his job. Erik was taking cues from Joe as though I was the threat.

It was amazing to me how quickly a dog knew to protect a kid, even if it were a game. Erik bonded with the kid, which is what I wanted. I wanted Erik to be able to sense danger but he probably did not need much help from me. I wanted Joe to know that Erik was his protector. It warms your heart to see such a bond.

Do you remember praising your dog for defending the kids, or playing as though they were?

Chapter Thirty-Three: Protecting Joe and Fridge Food

"He ain't heavy; he is my brother, Joe."
Joe and Erik at Clearwater Beach, Florida.
The sign said, "No Dogs Allowed" but Joe and Erik could not read the sign.

About the same period that I was playing the football game with Joe and Erik, when Joe was about 5 years old, the real protection drill paid off.

One Saturday afternoon, I had left home for a brief time. Beth was home with Joe. When I returned, Beth had a story to tell me.

Joe had been sitting on the ground at the bottom of the concrete steps which lead to our front door. In his hand was the end of the garden hose. Joe had turned on the water, used the end of the hose to drill holes into the dirt, and made a muddy, watery, mess. Erik was lying on the top step watching over Joe. Beth was somewhere in the house.

The solid front door was open, but the screen door was open so Beth could see and hear Joe if she needed.

Beth heard Erik bark in a manner she had never heard from him. It was a vicious sound. She had seen him fight and heard that sound, but this was different.

She ran to the door. Joe was still making his mud, drilling into the ground with the garden hose. Erik was standing at the street. A young black kid, about 11 years old, was standing petrified in the street. Erik was standing about 10 feet from the kid. The kid was holding boxes in his hands, balancing them against his chest.

Beth knew the kid was scared to death, but harmless. She called muddy Joe into the house, and then yelled at Erik to come into the house. Erik obeyed her, after turning and seeing that Joe was no longer behind him. Beth put Erik in the house with Joe, then approached the kid. He told Beth that he was selling cookies. Beth felt sorry for the kid; he did not live in this neighborhood and someone had dropped him off to sell cookies.

Beth did the right thing; she bought 3-4 boxes of cookies from the kid. She took the cookies into the house and promptly threw the cookies into the trash. She walked to the refrigerator, called Erik over, opened the refrigerator door, and looked for any type of treat she could feed him. He ate hot dogs, yogurt, cheese, and anything else she would give him, just like Brandy Middlebrooks had done. Erik knew how to stand in front of a refrigerator and eat if you would feed him. Beth loved him that day.

Beth was not overly affectionate to Erik, but loved him nonetheless. This day she treated him like a king. Joe was still a muddy mess, but it did not matter. Erik earned his stripes.

Do you remember when your dog unexpectedly defended a family member, especially a kid?

Chapter Thirty-Four: A Hospital Visit

Beth and I had separated during the marriage (I was a dummy), and she had moved into an apartment. I remained in the house. By this time, Erik was about 6 years old.

One weekend during the summer, I had to travel to Easley, SC to play in a softball tournament. I left on Friday to travel the 120 miles, and was to return sometime on Sunday. My friend Tom Burdyl was to check in on Erik, who had food and water outside the back door.

At about 3pm on Sunday, I drove to the front of my house. I did not see Erik, but that was of no consequence. As I stepped out of my car, a girl who was about 11 years old, and who I had never seen before, rode up to me on a bicycle.

"Have you seen Erik" the girl said.

"No, I just got home. I was out of town last night."

"He is up at Tommy's house, up the hill, and he is hurt."

How did she know Erik, and know where he lived, and know I was his owner, or where I lived?

I knew the name of the kid to whom she was referring, so now I had to go find Erik. This kid lived a few blocks from my house.

I drove up the hill, turned right, back to the left to the stop sign, turned right, traveled about two blocks, turned left, and about 3 houses down the street I slowed down. There he was, lying at the entrance gate to a huge yard. The gate was used for a car to enter the yard.

I pulled up alongside him and he stood. I could see his back-right leg was hurt. I picked him up and placed him into the car. He was breathing a bit rapidly, as if he was in pain.

After I arrived at my house, I carried him to the front porch, where I laid him down. I went in and got him some water and something out of the refrigerator for him to eat. As he was standing to eat, I reached around him and felt his leg. The lower portion of the leg was broken, flopping. I had to get him to the vet.

I knew where the weekend vet office was located because it was next to the post office I used. I carried him in, and the vet gave him a shot to knock him out. He looked dead; he felt dead. I felt dead. It was all I could do to keep from crying. This dog had gotten into trouble again, and now it was serious.

X-rays were taken. The vet told me he would need to have a spoon cast put on his leg for a while because they could not set the bone while the leg was swollen. The veterinarian put the cast on his leg, taped him up, and told me to be in touch with Erik's regular veterinarian.

Erik came out of the anesthesia, but was real drunk. I took him home, fed him anything he wanted (pizza was first preference) and he slept.

The next day I told Dr. Ray Elam, Erik's regular veterinarian, what had happened. Dr. Elam told me to keep Erik home for a few days, then bring him in when the swelling subsided. That was our plan, but not Erik's plan.

After the second day, after leaving Erik in the fenced in backyard, I came home from work to find Erik standing in the street near the neighbor's house.

It took a bit of coaxing, but I got him back into the house. I went into the back yard and found the escape route; he had dug under the fence at a moist area near a fresh water stream. That explained why his cast and the tape on the cast were wet. The cast had moved and was not supporting the leg since his foot was not cradled as was needed. There seemed to be some binding of tape against the skin.

I took him into the house and laid him on the kitchen floor. I put the back of my thigh over his torso and carefully took the tape off his cast. His leg was still broken, and it had to be painful, but if your dog trusts you he will let you attend to injuries. Erik was that way; the trust was enormous and he allowed me to re-tape his leg into the cast.

The next day I noticed swelling above the cast. The skin was hot. I thought it was infection of some kind. I took Erik to the vet, and learned that in fact the leg was infected, and had started to become gangrenous. I left him with the vet for a few days to allow the swelling to subside and treat him with antibiotics.

Joe was about two years old at that time. I took Joe to the vet to see Erik in the cage. That broke my heart. It is hard to see your young kid watch his buddy in a cage, and hurt.

Later in the week, the vet told me that Erik would not remain still long enough for the swelling to subside, so surgery was the only option. Erik was to have 4 tiny screws placed on a plate to hold the leg secure. I cannot remember how much that cost, but it had to have been outrageous.

A day or so after the surgery, he came home and was walking. I had less money.

Do you remember taking your dog to the emergency animal clinic, and the anxiety of this "doggie emergency room"?

Chapter Thirty-Five: A Dog Plans a Covert Attack

One late afternoon in the fall of 1982, I took Joe and Erik to a park. Erik would always want to go, and sometimes wander a bit but never became lost. I brought a soccer ball to kick with Joe. Soccer was not a big deal for me since I played baseball and football, but to a four-year-old kid, this was big time fun with your dad. A four-year-old kid is pretty easily entertained.

The park was not far from the house, so we walked. I did need to put Erik on a leash to get to the park but took it off when we arrived.

Joe and I began passing the ball back and forth, kicking it softly enough for Joe to handle. Then we began "dribbling" the ball down the field, advancing as we passed it to one another. Erik stood approximately 10 yards in front of me, crouching and barking as he was backing up at the same time. He would not stop. He hated what we were doing. Something about the ball being kicked back and forth bothered Erik.

I told Erik to stop barking, but he kept barking. Finally, I got the ball in front of me and yelled again. He kept barking. I then kicked the ball at him. The ball hit Erik squarely in the chest and knocked him backwards. It did not hurt him, but he was stunned. It shut him up. He walked to my right, out of view. I thought I had shut up that dog.

I got the ball back, and kicked it to Joe. We walked down the field a short distance, kicking the ball back and forth, when I felt something grab me and pinched me hard on the back of my left calf. I turned around and saw Erik standing about 4 yards from me.

I leaned over, pulled up the leg of my sweat pants, and saw that a trickle of blood was running down my calf. Then, I noticed a small tear in my sweat pants at the calf area. Erik was still standing, looking at me.

That dog got angry that I kicked him with the soccer ball because he would not stop barking. After being hit with the ball, Erik had circled around behind me, sneaked up on me, and bit my leg for hitting him with the soccer ball.

This took planning. This took forethought. I had never seen a dog put a plan together to avenge something, but he did. He would do something similar years later.

I had to laugh. I showed Beth the bite (it was a nick) and she thought it was what I deserved. At that moment, Erik was her friend. I was impressed that a dog could think that far ahead. I never kicked a ball at him after that. He made his point.

Did your dog ever appear to think out a plan more than a few steps ahead of simple immediate reaction?

Chapter Thirty-Six: Eating in the Car

During a criminal uncover assignment in Newberry, SC, I returned home every Friday morning after the third shift ended. I would go to the apartment, get Erik and some stuff, and head out.

Before I left town, I stopped at a fast food place and get sausage biscuits to eat on the way to Columbia. It was relaxing to drive and eat. Erik would be in the passenger seat, until the food arrived. After getting my food order, I put the bag of food on my lap to dig out the food. Erik would come across the seat and put his front paws on my right thigh; we were eye to eye. The first sausage biscuit would be his, always.

Do you remember driving while eating something which the dog wanted to share, or wanted you to share? The dog had to be fed first before you could enjoy your food. If you had kids in the car, it was a nightmare.

Chapter Thirty-Seven: Caged

In the Spring of 1983, Erik traveled with me on an undercover assignment at a manufacturing firm in Newberry, SC. My job was to infiltrate the plant and find out who was stealing what and who was dealing drugs. Erik had traveled on two prior assignments, lasting about 3 months each.

I was working a third shift assignment, sleeping during the day. My living accommodation was a house which was at least 100 years old, 3 stories high, and had been made into a rooming house. I left Erik out during the night. He was always home when I returned. It was kind of like he would sleep on the front porch to guard the house for all the tenants. They all knew him.

I had a roommate for a few months. He was a nice guy and needed a place to stay, so I rented him one of the rooms. He got along well with Erik.

One morning I returned to the apartment at about 6:30 a.m. and did not see Erik. At first I had no concern. After about 30 minutes, I became concerned.

I went outside and looked around. No dog. Since Erik was 9 years old, and had lost one testicle to cancer, I thought he had felt bad and crawled off to die. Yes, that came to mind.

The house in which I lived was elevated on bricks, so I looked under the house. I began calling to him. I drove around the neighborhood. I thought this was it, Erik had probably died. What a sad way to lose a dog, and what would I tell Joe?

After returning from driving around the neighborhood, I stood in the back of the house near the driveway. I just happened to look over into the back yard of the neighbor next door. I had never been over there, and really did not pay much attention to the yard.

As I casually looked across the back yard, something looked weird. There appeared to be a box of some kind in the grass on the opposite side of a flower bed, and it was about 30 yards from me. The box appeared to have wires on the side, and I could see something in the box.

I will never know why it got my attention. Whatever was in the box/cage appeared to be in silhouette, and I could not make it out. I pressed my lips together and pulled air between my lips, making the kissing sound which 90 percent of dogs respond by alerting. When I made that kissing sound, the silhouette in the box/cage moved. Oh, my God, is there an animal in that cage?

I jumped over a bricked area and got closer to the cage. IT WAS ERIK! Erik was in the cage. The cage was a trap. The cage had a rectangular front opening with a swinging gate-like door; the gate would be propped open, and the animal would enter the cage to get the food in the cage (I found a small open can of dog food, empty), and the gate would close. The animal was trapped, and it was Erik.

I leaned over to comfort him. He was very calm, as though he knew I was saving him. I pushed open the trap door after a minute of figuring out how the damned thing worked. Also, I was hoping the neighbor would not walk out and see me rescuing my dog from his trap.

Erik was free. He escaped another brush with his Maker.

We went back to the upstairs apartment and he was fed.

While Erik was eating, my roommate arrived. "Where is Erik" he said.

"He is in the kitchen, eating" I told him.

"Good, because I saw the dog catcher's truck pull up when I got out of my car."

I told him what happened. His reply was "What a dog you have."

Remember when your dog used up one of those favors God gave him?

Do you remember looking for your dog, and finding the dog either involved in mischief or trouble?

Chapter Thirty-Eight: The Dog Behind the Bus

In 1978, the Yankees won the World Series, Joe was born, and I was living in Pageland, SC, working at a bank. One of my co-workers, Steve Clark, would run with me during some mornings before work. We ran approximately four miles.

Beth was pregnant, and still teaching, so most weeks I left Erik in Columbia with her. A few weeks I took Erik to Pageland with me.

As Steve and I ran the regular route, we would come upon a school bus approximately one mile from the end of our run. Just like clockwork, a big boxer dog would appear from behind the bus and chase us down the road. I knew how to make that stop.

The following weekend, I brought Erik to Pageland with me.

The following Monday morning, Steve and I ran our route and had some company with us; Erik. I knew that boxer would be waiting for us. I showed up at the appointed place having Erik on a moderately long leash. Steve did not know Erik was going to join us, but that was not a problem. Erik kept up with us.

As we approached the school bus near the end of our run, I told Steve that if that boxer was nearby, he was going to get a surprise.

As we were passing the bus which was parked to our right, the boxer jumped out. Erik came to alert, and I dropped the leash. That boxer was surprised, and Erik was in his element.

Erik rushed toward the dog, made contact, a fight began, and the boxer quickly ran away. Erik caught back up with us, as his leash dragged on the ground. I picked up the leash and we laughed like crazy.

Do you remember how your dog defended you when he perceived a threat from another dog?

Yeah, My Dog Did That, Too

Chapter Thirty-Nine: Erik Attacks My Tie

Erik was affectionate, and enjoyed playing rough.
Joe ducks his head to keep from being bumped.

In the Spring of 1986, I made a professional leap and bought out an investigative firm which was being run by two former cops. The partners, Dave Lawrence and Jim Bartles, owned the company. After I bought their company, Dave stayed for a month so I could meet his regular clients. In the meantime, I hired a lady named C.J. Tinder, who has no investigative experience, and turned out to be one of the most intelligent and intuitive persons I ever met.

One afternoon, C.J. and I were returning to the office after photographing a wrecked automobile. Erik was at the veterinarian office getting a regular examination.

I decided to swing by and pick him up on the way back to my office. He had the regular checkup, bath, and that metal rod procedure. He was glad to see me, and knew that metal rod is part of the visit to the vet.

Erik did not need a leash to get into the car. I drove to the office and let Erik walk in with no leash. Erik was about 11 years old, and I figured he knew how to behave.

Erik, C.J., and I walked into the building and turned left to walk down the hall. I asked C.J. to open the door to let Erik walk in before us. We walked in as we heard Dave jump up from his desk after seeing a 75-pound dog walk in alone.

I could tell that Dave was a little nervous about Erik being in the office, so I decided to have some fun, at Dave's expense of course.

The office was small. The two desks were perpendicular to each other with about 4 feet of space between the corners of the desks, allowing access to our seats. Erik was lying down between the desks, and then the fun began.

I stood up from my chair, which made Erik stand. C.J. was seated directly in front of my desk. I gave C.J. a weird look, and then I looked at Erik. Silently, I raised my hands near my face, palms facing one another, and said to Erik, "Come on."

Erik knew this was going to be the "slap game" where I would square off with him; he would crouch and growl in a menacing, frightening manner. Erik knew the game, but if you had not seen it, you would be scared. Erik would appear to be so enraged, teeth showing, that you would think he was going to tear off my face. He knew that he was going to lunge at me, I would repel him by slapping his nose/mouth area, and if I could score 10 hits before he either bit me or grabbed any particle of clothing, or bit my hand, I would win. I probably won 70 percent of the time, but he was very quick. After either of us won, I would tell him to sit, and he would stop immediately. He would offer alternate paws to shake hands, I would then lean over to let him lick the side of my face, and the game would be over. It really was a good agility drill, but Dave thought Erik had lost his ever-loving mind.

I moved around a bit in the cramped office so Erik could lunge at me. By this time, Dave had gotten up from his chair and was backed against the wall. (I am laughing as I write).

"What is he doing" Dave asked.

As I held up my hands and enticed Erik, he lunged at me a few times and I "popped him" on the nose area. All the time I was watching Dave and trying not to laugh.

I had popped Erik a few times and had not been bitten. Then, I leaned over to pop him as he had all four feet on the floor. As I slowly stood up, Erik jumped up and bit the Pierre Cardin tie I was wearing. He bit the tie right in the middle of the logo. I was not expecting this. Erik clamped on to the tie, and the weight of the dog caused me to fall forward. Erik landed back on his four feet, and our faces were about a foot apart, and we were eyeball-to-eyeball as my tie was in his mouth.

C.J. was laughing out loud. Dave was still up against the wall.

Erik had won, we laughed at Dave, but Erik got the last laugh.

After he knew he had won, I said "sit" and let released my tie. I shook both his paws, he licked my face, and it was over.

I kept that tie for at least a year after that incident. The tie had tooth marks on it. It was a reminder from Erik that he had won that round.

Do you remember when your dog grabbed your clothing to send you a message?

Chapter Forty: Getting Older; Sad Signs

When we moved to our new house, I created an office above the garage. There were steps, maybe 15 or 20, leading to the work area above the garage.

Tom and Laurette Burdyl would drop off their dogs (Orbit and Pluto) when they went out of town. They were great dogs to have around, and you could see the connection of dog friends. Even though Pluto (a male) was younger and now stronger, Pluto never challenged Erik for food or anything. One night I stood in the driveway with a box of dog biscuits, and each dog would take their turn getting biscuits. I would look at each dog, call their name and make them "speak." The funny thing was Pluto would not speak; he made a sound like he was sneezing. I gave him the biscuits anyway.

Erik was about 12 years old when we moved into the new house. His hips seemed to bother him.

Just before we moved, Joe and I were playing with a football at a high school football field. We walked to the field, and of course, Erik was with us. I noticed that Erik was not running much; he was almost limping as he slowly walked. He appeared to be in some discomfort. It was evident in his face.

As we were walking home, Erik walked behind us. That was unusual. He was off the leash, but he would still try to keep up. This time he could not. I could tell he did not want to walk the ¾ of a mile home. I knew the signs. It was breaking my heart.

I handed the football to Joe, picked up Erik, and carried him home. In my heart, I knew what was happening. The vet had told me that he was having hip problems, and this was common with dogs of German Shepherd, collie, retriever breeds.

We gave him pills the vet gave us. I was never sure if they worked.

It was good to have friends like Orbit and Pluto with him as he was older. Dogs know the signs.

Do you remember when the body was giving out, and you lived with the thought of losing your dog?

Chapter Forty-One: The Last Days

I was always amazed how dogs would come into a room and lie next to us, just wanting to be near us.

In the spring of 1986, I could bear it no longer. I knew he was in pain, and not having fun anymore. He hesitated to climb any steps.

Joe attended an elementary school which was 2 blocks from our house. After school, Joe came home and Erik would be there. Joe had two babysitters; Harry Cary (the announcer for the Chicago Cubs) and Erik, who had been Joe's companion for 8 years. Joe was safe for the hour or so before Beth arrived home from her teaching job.

Spring break was beginning for Beth (a school teacher) and Joe (a third grader). On the Sunday before the break began, I told Beth I was going to do some work in the yard. Erik went outside with me. I took a shovel and started digging a hole in the back corner of the yard. An empty wooden box in which a heat exchanger was delivered was under the house, and I dug the hole large enough to accommodate the heat exchanger box.

Beth came outside and asked what I was doing with the box. I carried the box to the hole and told her it was for Erik. I could see in her face she was shocked, and she said, "Don't tell me that." I told her that tomorrow was the day Erik was to be "put down" and end his pain. She knew, but we also had to tell Joe.

She left, and I finished digging the grave. Nothing more was said until the next morning. I cannot remember that night. My memory has always been very sharp, but that night was a blur.

I called the vet early that next morning. It was Monday. It was better for them to be home and not go with me.

I put a thick bedspread into my van. I picked up Erik, placed him on the bedspread, and drove to the vet. Beth called my friend Tom, and told Tom what was happening. Tom had been around Erik from the college days when Erik was a puppy. Tom's dogs, Orbit and Pluto, played with Erik and they were together a lot because we visited on another's houses.

Moments after arriving at the vet office, Tom pulled into the parking lot next to me. He and I could not make eye contact. We were both holding back our emotions, trying to be tough guys, but the loss of a dog will break most men.

I walked to the back of the van, opened the doors, and started to carry Erik into the building when I heard a voice behind me. It was Dr. Elam, the veterinarian. Dr. Elam told me we could do this out here. He had a syringe in his hand. I knew what it was for.

I sat in the back of the van. My legs were hanging over the rear bumper. I cradled Erik onto my lap. Erik was comfortable lying on my lap. He was calm. He knew he was with me. I stroked his head. He trusted me; he always did.

I knew I had to do this. I became stone faced, and it was like an out of body experience. I knew if I became emotional I would lose control. I have no idea how I kept from crying.

Dr. Elam asked to position Erik so I could give access to a front leg. Dr. Elam took the leg in his hand, and inserted a needle into a vein. Erik jumped a little, but I was holding him tightly so he would not move much. Dr. Elam said Erik would slowly pass out. As Dr. Elam pushed the plunger on the syringe, Erik squirmed a bit; then he relaxed. Fewer than 15 seconds later, Erik was dead.

I thanked Dr. Elam. There was no charge. I could not look at Tom, and I knew Tom would not look at me.

I wrapped Erik into the bedspread and drove back to the house. Tom drove behind me. I could see that Tom had turned on his headlights as though he was in a funeral procession. I guess he was; his friend had died too.

When I arrived at my house, Beth and Joe came out to the van. I let them see Erik and they both touched his head. I still had not cried, thinking, " I had to get through this."

I carried Erik to the grave which I had dug the day before. I placed his body into the box, still covered by the bedspread. Beth stood next to Joe, hugging Joe as Joe watched me lay his friend into the ground.

Joe's friend was gone. Erik understood Joe as none of us did. Erik taught Joe about courage and loyalty. Erik knew to oversee Joe if neither I nor Beth were nearby. Joe lost his buddy; a buddy who bonded immediately with the infant Joe, a friend who slept under Joe's crib, helped him learn to walk, protected, and loved him.

I know you remember the day you lost your four-legged friend.

Chapter Forty-Two: Dogs Teach Us How to Love

When we get a dog, our first thought is not that we will outlive the dog, but during the life of the dog, we know it is true. Many people get dogs when they are young, or have kids. After the kids are grown, and the dog who played with our kids is no longer here, we rarely go out and get another dog. Our reasoning is "This will be the last one. They are a lot of trouble. They keep me from being able to travel. I have to run back to the house and feed the dog."

Funny, we never made those excuses when the kids were around, or when we were young ourselves. Yes, we had to change our lives to attend to our dogs, but dogs changed our lives for the better, and we are better persons because we loved the dogs and let the dogs love us until the end.

This is Joe and his dad on Joe's first Easter. Erik was Joe's buddy, watching him grow.
Beth and I relied upon Erik to help protect this kid.

Joe, and all kids, learn things from their dogs which parents cannot teach.

When your dog is gone, you miss everything your dog did, both the good and the bad. Somehow the stinky baths, the turned over trash can, illness, dog catcher, chewed shoe, jumping on the bed when very dirty, or taking food off your plate, are all forgotten when your dog gives you a kiss or jumps into your lap. The relationship a dog has with a kid growing up is special. The relationship with an older person is special. There are so many different things that all dogs do, and if you give them a chance, they will do one thing that they all do; that is love you unconditionally.

J.B. Simms

www.ingramcontent.com/pod-product-compliance
Lightning Source LLC
Chambersburg PA
CBHW080520300426
44112CB00018B/2805